Learning
to
Listen

LEARNING
TO
LISTEN

Revised Edition

**A book by mothers for mothers
of hearing-impaired children**

Edited by Pat Vaughan

Voice for Hearing-Impaired Children

*With a Foreword by David Mitchell, M.D., F.R.C.S. (C)
Otolaryngologist-in-Chief
Hospital for Sick Children
Associate Professor, Otolaryngology
University of Toronto*

Beaufort Books, Inc.
New York   Toronto

Library of Congress Cataloging in Publication Date

Main entry under title:
Learning to listen.

   1. Children, Deaf — Longitudinal studies. 2. Deaf — Means of
communication — Longitudinal studies. 3. Children, Deaf — Family
Relationships — Longitudinal studies. I. Vaughan, Pat.
HV2465.L4 1981   371.91'23   81-4938
ISBN 0-8253-0065-7   AACR2

Beaufort Books, Inc.
9 East 40th St.,
New York, N.Y.
10016

Published in Canada by General Publishing Co. Limited

Printed in Canada

10 9 8 7 6 5 4 3 2 1

Dedicated to

Louise Crawford

from

the parents, children, and teachers

she has taught

to listen

FOREWORD

Helen Keller has been quoted as saying that if she had a choice she would have preferred the sense of hearing to that of vision. The fine art of communication which man has developed is the major skill which separates human beings from other species. It is obvious to most that, without the ability to communicate, our modern industrial society could not have evolved.

When parents are told that their child has a significant hearing handicap they frequently experience a profound sense of disappointment with the realization that the future of their child may be limited. There is no doubt in the minds of many of those who work with hearing-impaired children that the diagnosis of hearing loss creates severe stress on the family unit. Yet some of the children born with this problem grow to become accomplished members of society, communicating effectively and leading essentially normal lives. In fact, most hearing-handicapped people raise healthy families and show a better work record than many of their normal-hearing peers.

The hearing-impaired adult who has been successfully integrated into society is usually the product of many hours of hard work and discipline, particularly on the part of his parents and the educators who diligently labor to improve the communication skills which are so naturally attained by the normal-hearing child.

To communicate by voice through hearing the spoken word is the ultimate hope of any hearing-impaired individual. In this book we see a documentation of auditory training as a method of teaching a child speech and language skills. The authors are parents of children who have indeed developed communication skills despite severe hearing loss.

These parents recall the deep sense of hopelessness which enveloped them when they first discovered their children had a hearing problem.

They attempt to communicate their experiences and their sense of accomplishment as their children gradually developed the ability to communicate with society. They relate, both through personal example and through the documentation of teaching methods, how their children have successfully coped with a major handicap.

This book is as much a tribute to the parents of these hearing-impaired children as it is to the teacher, Miss Louise Crawford, who assisted them.

David P. Mitchell, M.D., F.R.C.S. (C)
Otolaryngologist-in-Chief
Hospital for Sick Children
Associate Professor, Otolaryngology
University of Toronto

ACKNOWLEDGMENTS

In thanking the many persons involved in the production of this book, I feel it is appropriate to explain how the idea for such a book came about.

In June, 1973, Frederick F. Hewer, Principal of Salem Public School in Wellington County, the father of a pre-school hearing-impaired child, was killed in a car accident. His widow, Julie Hewer, in appreciation of her husband's enthusiasm for auditory training, requested that the memorial tributes given to the Canadian Hearing Society be used to help parents like themselves who do not live near an auditory training clinic but would like their hearing-impaired children to learn to listen. Mrs. Hewer felt she and her husband would have welcomed guidance in their early days of coping with their daughter's handicap.

Thus, on October 9, 1974, we six mothers were called to a meeting at the Canadian Hearing Society. Mrs. Hewer's idea was explained to us and the project put into our hands. This book slowly evolved over several months of telephone conversations, afternoon coffee visits and spirited evening meetings.

As editor, I first wish to thank the mothers—Earlene Wasik, Donna Wilk, Ariella Samson, Doreeen Humphreys and Cathy Constantinidis — for their enthusiastic co-operation and their ideas; and especially for their time. For any mother of a hearing-impaired child, every minute counts and there are few minutes to spare.

Secondly, I wish to thank those doctors and teachers who contributed material for the book: Dr. David Mitchell for the foreword and Dr. Donald Hood for supplying audiograms; Miss Louise Crawford for her chapter "Auditory Training—A Teacher's Approach."

For the production, special thanks to Barrie Martland and Stephen

*Pepper of Marpep Publishing Limited for the typesetting and layout; to
Jules Samson for photography; Bev. Shaw, Barbara Nethercol and Winara
Schneider for typing, and Gore and Storrie Consulting Engineers for
allowing us to use their duplicating facilities.*

*Finally, I wish especially to thank Mrs. Dorothy Scott, who, in
addition to contributing two chapters, and the glossary and bibliography
spent many many hours with me painstakingly reviewing every word and
idea in the text; and especially for egging and prodding me on. So
enthusiastic was she to see this project completed that she even
conscripted her friend, Dr. Margaret Noble, Oxford England, who came
to Canada for a holiday, to do some collating and proofreading! Working
with Mrs. Scott has been an invaluable learning experience.*

*Mrs. Joan Beattie, president of the Canadian Hearing Society, also
merits special thanks for her assistance in the publication of this book.*

*All of us who have worked on this book feel privileged that we have
been able, in some small way, to contribute to the fruition of Mrs.
Hewer's idea.*

*P.V.
May, 1976*

Many people are to be thanked for this second edition of Learning to Listen:
*firstly, Ariella Samson, Donna Wilk, Doreen Humphreys, Earlene Wasik,
and Cathy Constantinidis, the mothers who, with their customary enthusiasm,
updated their children's stories; secondly, Louise Crawford, Dorothy Scott,
Warren Estabrooks, and Dorothy Boothroyd, dedicated teachers who are
always so willing to share their techniques, experiences and insights; thirdly,
the Canadian Hearing Society, especially Brian Hunter who was most
generous with his time and always available when assistance was needed;
and last, but not least, Voice for Hearing Impaired Children, and particularly
Jules Samson and John Craig who, because of their commitment to the
auditory approach, ensured that this book would be printed again.*

All of us involved feel gratified that Learning to Listen *has become an
invaluable teaching aid for parents and teachers alike.*

*P.V.
June, 1981.*

Contents

Part I

The mothers' own stories

Jonathan 1

Vanessa 7

Richard 17

Peter 27

Matthew 33

John 41

Part II

Auditory training

Through lessons at home 51

A teacher's approach — by Louise Crawford . . 75

Through daily routines 87

Through books 101

Can include nursery school 111

Part III

An audiogram

What does it mean? 119

Hearing aids

Success depends on good aids 125

Keeping the aid in good working order 127

Part IV

In summary

A teacher listened, too — by Dorothy Scott . . 137

A mother's pledge — by Sally Farr 142

Part V

Five years later
The children 145
Auditory training
A teacher's update — by Louise Crawford . . 169
Lessons with older children —
by Warren Estabrooks 171
Using the telephone —
by Dorothy Boothroyd 175
Parents, be aware! — by Dorothy Scott . . . 177
Hearing aids today 179

Part VI

Services available 185
Bibliography 188
Glossary 193

Introduction

We all react differently when we learn that our child's hearing is impaired. Some of us cry uncontrollably while others are numbed by the news. Some of us are relieved that our child's problem has been finally diagnosed because we have suspected for some time that "something is wrong". Most of us at some time feel a great sense of guilt—"It's our fault, we did something wrong." At other times we feel great anger—"Why did this have to happen to us?" Almost all of us feel deep sadness and an overwhelming anxiety about our child's future. "What does 'profound hearing loss' or 'profoundly deaf' or 'severely hearing impaired' mean as far as my child is concerned?"

Unfortunately, when your child is first diagnosed, there is no real answer to this question. However, there is one thing that is very important for you to understand about your child, no matter how his hearing loss has been described. **HE OR SHE PROBABLY HAS SOME HEARING.** Less than five percent of children diagnosed as hearing impaired have no hearing at all. The idea of total deafness or being "stone deaf" is a thing of the past.

Teachers and doctors who work with hearing impaired children have found that many children, even those thought to be profoundly deaf, can use the little bit of hearing they have to quite an extraordinary degree; and that those children who use this little bit of hearing (technically called "residual hearing") can develop better language and clearer and more natural speech than those who do not use it. However, the hearing impaired child has to be taught to use this hearing. He has to learn to listen. And the only people who can really help him to do this are you, his parents, particularly his mother.

"How can my child learn to listen?" you are no doubt asking. "What can I do?" Auditory Training is the formal name for the process of teaching a hearing impaired child to listen and to use his residual hearing in the language learning process. Don't be frightened by this name!

Auditory Training is really quite simple: much of it can be done naturally at home as you and your child carry out daily routines. The purpose of this book is to show you how it can be done. Once you begin to think about it, you will realize it is what any mother of any "normal" child does unconsciously all the time.

When the idea of a book to introduce parents to auditory training was conceived at the Canadian Hearing Society, it was felt even by teachers of hearing impaired children, that the best persons to write about it were the persons actually doing it day in and day out with their children, i.e. mothers. Consequently, this book is mainly a book by mothers for mothers, with some chapters contributed by teachers.

Six mothers (myself included) who have been involved in the Auditory Training program at the Hospital for Sick Children have written of their experiences in teaching their own children. We hope our candid stories of our successes and frustrations will assist you to help your child develop language.

As you read the mothers' stories, you will no doubt feel "This isn't simple at all!" And you're right. While auditory training itself is not complicated, what is difficult is the energy, persistence, imagination and creativity to make it work.

"Why am I the only one who can help my child develop his listening skills? Can't a teacher do it?" you may be wondering.

Certainly, a teacher's guidance is valuable, but a teacher couldn't possibly do the whole job for many reasons. A normally hearing child begins to learn language the day he is born, even though he may not begin talking for one, two, or even in some cases, three years; and he learns language all his waking hours in a close, loving relationship with a mother who babbles with him, coos at him, sings to him and talks to him. The hearing impaired child needs the same kind of stimulation and warmth which only his mother can provide.

This book is not intended as a course in auditory training with a step-by-step description of what to do next. Rather, it is designed to give you a feeling for auditory training—it will explain how you can turn almost every experience into an auditory and language building experience for your child.

Auditory training as the mothers involved in this book see it is many things. It is planning and carrying out language lessons with your child on a regular basis. It is talking to your child all day long and making the most of everyday routines to develop his language. It is involvement of the whole family. It is, above all, an attitude or frame of mind—an attitude that the child is a "listening child", that he uses his hearing, even though it is imperfect, ALL THE TIME, just as any normal child does.

It is unlikely that any of the children described in this book will ever have to attend a special school for the deaf. They will be able to go to the same schools as their hearing brothers and sisters. They may need extra help from mother at home and perhaps from a tutor or in a special class within a regular school. But no matter where or how a child is formally educated, he cannot possibly be harmed by the type of auditory training described here. You and your child have nothing to lose by trying it.

Although we have said this book is not a step-by-step course, after reading it you will certainly understand where and how to begin. And the time to begin is now; today if possible. The earlier auditory training is begun, the more successful it is likely to be.

We would like to emphasize that, although all of us find that auditory training is hard work, a great deal of it is just plain fun. As you try many of the ideas and games suggested here, you will very quickly discover that the same can be true for you.

PAT VAUGHAN, Editor

Part I

The mothers' own stories

Jonathan

Vanessa

Richard

Peter

Matthew

John

Jonathan

*Jonathan is now four years old and soon will
be starting Junior Kindergarten, his second year
in a school with normally hearing children. He
enjoys school and gets along well with other
children. He tests as being "profoundly deaf".
He has been fitted binaurally for the last two
years. His mother stopped working shortly before
his birth and decided not to return when his
impairment was diagnosed. The family is now
expecting their second child. English is both
parents' second language.*

It was a month before Jonathan's first birthday that we
were finally told that Jonathan was profoundly deaf. I say
"finally" because that was our immediate response to the
news, before my tears did indeed gush out. For eight long
months we carried the fear within us, had it dispelled by
our pediatrician, relatives and friends, and yet the fear and
suspicions remained. It was a fact now, and even as the
tears flowed, my first reactions were: "Now that we know,
we *can* finally do something. It's time to stop feeling sorry
for ourselves, and time to begin doing something for Jonathan!"

When two weeks later the earmould was ready and a
hearing aid was given to us on loan, we had already made
some decisions. Our decisions were based on a few books
we had read, among them Doreen Pollack's *Educational
Audiology For The Limited Hearing Infant*. The most
important thing we learned from our reading was: **the
responsibility was ours.**

Talk, talk, talk was the advice we brought home from
the hospital that first day with the hearing aid. And talk I
did, watching all the while for a light of recognition in
Jonathan's eyes. But nothing was different really, except
that I ran out of something to say constantly. And every
time Jonathan blinked, I thought "he heard that!" But he

1

blinked all the time, whether I said something or not. Not too much happened to Jonathan that first day, but I went to bed that night too tired to feel disappointed.

Because I had to talk four to eight inches from the hearing aid, and since Jonathan wasn't walking yet I learned to crawl all over again so I could stay close to him. It was a warm Spring, and I was in shorts most of the time, and for the next few months the scabs on my knees always got a second look everywhere.

Although he seemed oblivious to the hearing aid while wearing it, by the third day we began to notice differences in Jonathan's behavior. He became less active, and what seemed even worse to us at the time, less vocal as well. His babbling, which until now was our source of reassurance, though entirely lacking in all the consonants, gradually disappeared. It was only months later that I learned the obvious: **you have to be quiet in order to listen.** And there was a whole new world of sound out there to listen to.

Our first "big" response came on the tenth day. While Jonathan's back was turned to me, I crawled over to him while my fists literally pounded on the floor. It was a strange sensation for me, but for the first time ever, Jonathan turned around! We played this game over and over for days and we both loved every minute of it. Four days later, while we were both quite close to the front door, someone sounded the brass knocker outside unexpectedly and Jonathan turned to me anticipating our game. It was a long time before I remembered to open the front door in my excitement.

Two weeks passed by now, and once again Jonathan began babbling. Our formal lessons too were begun. Because it was hard to keep Jonathan in one place, our home lessons became "portable". We were seldom far from each other; either I crawled around Jonathan, or carried him about with me. I began to say the word "listen" anytime I heard something and gesture to my ear at the same time. What I really wanted was to train Jonathan to learn to

2

point to his own ear whenever he heard something. This also helped locate the source of most environmental sounds for him that until now I took for granted, such as the telephone, a barking dog, or an airplane flying overhead. The little bus that I pushed along the floor or across his high chair during mealtime went "bu bu bu bu", and the airplane went "ah———" as it flew up and down around us. The cat said "meow" to Jonathan, while the rabbit "hop hop" hopped about the place. And while I just talked and talked, Jonathan looked and smiled until one day while driving in the car I told him for the thousandth time about the airplane that went "ah———", and a small voice from the back seat answered "ah———". We then began as many voice games as I could think of. I would imitate Jonathan's vocal sounds and laughter as a feedback of his own voice and motivation to eventually do the same to mine.

By now, the hearing aid became the focal point of Jonathan's curiosity and he constantly removed the earmould. There were few remedies that we didn't try but the only one that finally did work was a light cotton hat with ear flaps which Jonathan then wore for the next three months, through the hottest part of summer, before he was able to leave the earmould alone.

We had a busy summer that year. Jonathan began walking; it was a little harder now to stay close to him. Our first trip outdoors with Jonathan was a very emotional one for us. Jonathan was only wearing his hearing aid for three days when we first took him to the park, and as far as we were concerned, everyone was all eyes. I was prepared to outstare everyone in my anger when I realized that no more attention was paid to him than to any other child. In fact it was quite some time before a young girl approached us to ask why Jonathan wore "that thing" in his ear. Once the tension was gone, it was really quite easy to answer that it helped him hear just like glasses helped others to see better. It was an attitude that has since helped set the mood with people we have come in contact with. Having established the fact that with his hearing aid Jonathan does

3

hear, he has been treated as a normal child ever since. It has also taught us that to a large extent other people's attitudes depend largely upon ours. The same has held true with our families and friends, and except for the initial "training" period, this has worked out for the best.

It was around this time as well that we decided that the more like any other child Jonathan looked, the more naturally he would be treated back. It was not for reasons of vanity alone that I discarded the hearing aid harness and replaced it with patch pockets which I sewed on the outside of all of Jonathan's outfits, as high up on his chest as possible, in direct line with his own voice. **If I expected people to talk as naturally to my deaf child as they would to any other normal hearing child, the paraphernalia of deafness had to disappear.** Eventually, this served the same purpose in our own household. Once the hearing aid was snuggly tucked into his pocket, I too forgot its presence. It

JONATHAN'S AUDIOGRAM

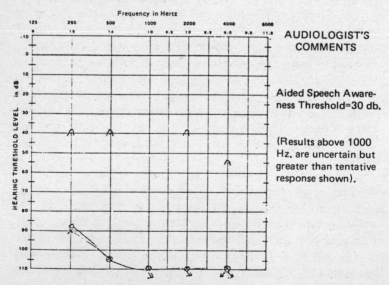

AUDIOLOGIST'S COMMENTS

Aided Speech Awareness Threshold=30 db.

(Results above 1000 Hz. are uncertain but greater than tentative response shown).

Jonathan's audiogram shows him as very profoundly deaf. He has essentially no measurable hearing in the higher frequencies yet is aware of speech throughout the range when using his aid.

no longer intimidated me and I could talk to Jonathan without the slightest effort.

Our lessons were still quite unstructured, mainly because of Jonathan's young age. But once my 'talk' habit was established, our lessons really lasted most of the day. Each week I would select certain useful words and repeat these in proper situations constantly. I would use them in as many ways as possible. This same list was gently pushed on anyone who stayed more than five minutes in our apartment, so that the lesson was reinforced as often as possible. When a year and a half later Jonathan began pointing to objects himself and asking "What's that?" it was the result of countless hours of conditioning.

In a month came Jonathan's first consonant, when everything on wheels became a "bu bu bu", and for days that was all we heard to our greatest joy. His vocabulary still only consisted of two words, "ah ———" for airplane, and "bu bu bu" for bus, but his comprehension was growing daily. "Moo" clearly meant a cow, and "bye bye" a wave of the hand. With six to eight animals and objects lined up in front of us, the responses were becoming more accurate daily; to a "meow" Jonathan picked up the cat unerringly, and for "hop hop" the rabbit. Weekly the list grew. And for each correct response I clapped my hands and shouted "Hurray!". It took only a couple of weeks before Jonathan would beat me each time with a clap and a hurray for himself. It was at this point in time too that Jonathan began to recognize his name and turn when called.

The record player kept us busy for long intervals. We began marching in time to the music, with Dad, or any other person whose services I could conscript, beginning and stopping the music to verbal signals of 'stop' and 'go'. It was indeed a difficult game to bring to an end. Much of our day was spent with books too. This was always an ideal way in which to reinforce vocabulary. Sitting in my lap and looking at the pictures I held, Jonathan learned to listen without any clues but the auditory ones.

5

On our first re-evaluation test at the hospital, the results of our talk campaign were quite obvious. His speech had grown, though only the two of us understood him:

ah———	was	*airplane*
bu bu bu	was	*bus*
bob	was	*bottle*
ba	was	*ball*
boo	was	*book*
ba ba	was	*bye bye*
bow bow	was	*dog*
ay	was	*hi*
ou	was	*out*
babbi	was	*baby*

But his comprehension extended to:

hop, hop
moo
flower
meow
stop
round and round
nose
eyes
tongue

We were on the first leg of our journey.

Vanessa

Vanessa is now five-and-a-half years old and tests as being "profoundly deaf". She attends Kindergarten at her local public school and her teacher feels that she gets along as well as her hearing classmates. Vanessa has a three-year-old brother. Her mother worked part-time before her hearing loss was diagnosed but since they began auditory training she has not been employed outside the home.

Vanessa received her hearing aid when she was 18 months old. I was terribly naive about deafness when she was diagnosed; so naive, in fact, that I thought all we had to do was put a hearing aid on her and that she would hear and understand things. I can remember how shocked I was when she first began to wear her aid. She was no different than she was before—she did not turn around when I called her name, she didn't look up when the telephone rang, she didn't run joyfully to the front door when I said "Daddy's home". She still screamed or pointed to indicate her wants and needs, took no notice of any sounds around her and was otherwise silent. What I didn't realize at the very beginning but very quickly came to understand was that although Vanessa was 18 months old, she was like a newborn infant in terms of hearing and language development. While her brain no doubt registered some sounds very shortly after she began to wear her aid, these sounds meant no more to her than the sounds a newborn infant hears mean to him.

Fortunately, not long after Vanessa began to wear her aid, we were contacted by the teacher at the Hospital for Sick Children. Vanessa was to start auditory training that week.

I had never heard of "auditory training" before. In fact, the term rather frightened me. However, at our first

7

meeting, the teacher was very relaxed and explained that we were simply going to teach Vanessa to listen and to use her hearing. She instructed me to buy a toy airplane, a bus, duck, cow, rabbit, cat, dog, sheep and baby chick because she would begin by working on the sounds associated with these—"bu bu bu" for the bus; "ah———" for the airplane; "quack quack" for the duck; "meow" for the cat; etc. Her other instructions were to babble baby sounds a great deal while we played and to talk, talk, talk, just as one would talk to any baby. However, we were to try to talk close to the hearing aid as much as possible because the best and clearest amplification occurs when the speaker's mouth is four to eight inches from the hearing aid microphone.

As a result of this first meeting, "auditory training" became a way of life for Vanessa and me, and my husband as well. I would try to do a short formal lesson with her every day similar to the lesson her teacher did (see pages 75-86); but in addition, we spent the whole day playing and doing things together so that she would be close to me as I babbled and talked and reinforced the sounds and words being worked on in her formal lessons. I became aware that my whole house was a potential "learning machine". I put pictures of the lesson words all over the house—on the kitchen wall, on the wall going up the staircase, on the wall around her crib, in the bathroom—so that we could look at them and talk about them together many many times a day.

Everytime we went up or down stairs, I would carry her, stop as we came to each picture and say something like "Here's a dog . . . bow wow, bow wow . . . the dog says bow wow, bow wow." I would repeatedly call her attention to sounds around the house such as the telephone ringing, the tea kettle whistling, etc. For example, everytime the telephone rang, I would pick her up, take her over to the telephone, point to my ear and then her ear and say "Listen! Telephone's ringing, I have to answer it." I let her help me with all the household tasks—washing floors, dusting, laundry, cooking, baking—and as you can imagine, she loved to help. As we "worked" (none of my

8

housework ever really got done, needless to say), I talked to her in simple phrases and sentences, describing what we were doing. "Vanessa, let's wash the floor ... Look ... It's dirty ... Really dirty ... Let's make it clean ... Here's the water ... etc. etc." Even washing her hands became a language lesson. I would show her the dirt on her hands and say "Vanessa, your hands are dirty ... Let's wash them ... Up on the chair ... Up, up, up ... Now you can reach ... Turn on the water ... water ... Oh! oh! oh! Too hot ... Now it's warm ... Nice and warm ... Here's the soap ... Vanessa's washing her hands ... Rub, rub, rub ... All dry ... Down, we go" etc. I would talk in the same way every time I washed her hands so that the same language would be repeated over and over again. I used all the events in the day to feed in language in this manner. Every morning we'd do "Daddy's going to work ... Bye bye Daddy; Bye bye ... Daddy's all gone ... All gone ... Daddy went bye bye" as we watched Daddy's car disappear around the corner.

It became extremely fatiguing and difficult to keep talking in this monologue fashion after a time because Vanessa never said anything. I was not sure that she was hearing what I was saying. However, I knew that no matter how frustrating it was for me to talk to someone who never responded, I had to do it. **She had to be bathed in sound and language, just as any newborn is.**

Two weeks after our first visit with the teacher, Vanessa began to babble ————"mamama", just as a young infant might babble, i.e. it did not mean "Mommy". I responded very enthusiastically and encouraged her to babble more. Soon "mamama" replaced screaming for many things she wanted. For example, when she wanted a drink of water, she would go to the sink and say "mamama". Once she started this, I responded not with babbling but with "Water ... Vanessa wants water ... Here's your water ... Drink the water ... Water's all gone ... etc."

Four weeks later, Vanessa was able to point to a bus when she heard me or her teacher say "bu bu bu" or to an airplane when we said "ah ———". She did not have to see our faces to make this discrimination. She could do it using only her hearing. Vanessa did not say these sounds at this time. She was in the program six months before she began to say the sounds at home, and it was nine months before she would say them with the teacher. **As with hearing children, her understanding of what was said preceded speech by many months.** To me it seemed that picking up the bus when she heard "bu bu bu" was the key that opened the door. She now attached meaning to sounds. And I knew for sure that she could hear something and was encouraged to keep on working with her in the same way.

After that her language began to grow. Reasonably quickly she learned to recognize, through hearing alone, all the animal sounds on which we had been working. New words were introduced; e.g. *flower, shoe, ball.* Also simple concept words were slowly introduced into lessons—*all gone, empty, hot* and *cold, round and round, up* and *down, stop* and *go, fast* and *slow.* I continued to teach her just as I had at the beginning with a short formal lesson daily and then talking and playing most of the day.

When Vanessa was two years old I was well advanced into my second pregnancy and was unable to carry her around as much and indulge in the physical games she liked to play, so at this time I began to do a great deal of drawing with her. I was a dreadful artist but she loved to sit on my knee at the table while I drew simple pictures to illustrate words and concepts and talked into the hearing aid microphone without having her watch my face. For example, I would draw a cup and say, "Here's a cup . . . See the cup". Then I'd touch it and say "Ow . . . it's hot" and rub my fingers. Then I'd say something like "Let's blow on it . . . Blow it . . . Touch it again . . . Now it's not hot." She enjoyed these drawing sessions so much that we were able to spend half to three-quarters of an hour at a time often two or three times a day doing this. And as time went on, the pictures became more and more complex—Mommy and Vanessa going shopping in the car,

Vanessa swinging, Daddy watching television, Daddy mowing the lawn, Vanessa helping Mommy bake a cake, etc.

Another thing that we began at this time and did a great deal of when she was between the ages of two and three was looking at books and magazines together. I used to sit in a rocking chair with Vanessa on my lap facing away from me and again I would talk about the pictures over her shoulder so that my mouth was the recommended four to eight inches from the hearing aid. We began with simple pictorial dictionary books (Richard Scarry's *Best Word Book Ever* was one of her favorites) and gradually moved on to simple story books such as the Small Family series by Lois Lenski. (A list of books the mothers have found to be useful in working with young children is given on pages 101-110). As we looked at the pictures, I would often attempt to dramatize in some way the one we were looking at. For example, if we were looking at a flower, I would say "Pretty flower . . . Let's smell it . . . Smell the flower" and I'd raise the book so we could smell the flower. Then I'd say "Let's pick the flower" and pretend to pick it. "Vanessa, you pick the flower . . . Let me smell it" and so on.

Through drawing and reading in this way Vanessa learned very early about pretending and this helped me greatly in expanding her language. Even before she was three, she would initiate little pretend dramas many times a day. For example, she'd come up to me and pretend to pass me something. I would pretend to take it, act very pleased and say something like, "Oh! a flower . . . What a pretty flower . . . I love flowers . . . Let's smell it . . . Here, you smell it . . . The flower needs water . . . Let's put it in some water." I'd get a small jar and fill it with water and then say, "Oh! doesn't that look pretty . . . So pretty . . . Let's put it on the table . . . There, it's on the table . . . Such a pretty flower." She just loved this type of game and would chuckle when we finished. After all, there was no flower really! Weren't we being silly!

I must point out that while we played such games over

and over again and they were very verbal games (i.e. I talked) Vanessa herself did not talk much. All she could say around the age of two-and-a-half to three was "Gaga ow", which meant, "Vanessa has a flower." Her comprehension was far greater than what she actually said. This is true for all children. **A baby understands a great deal of language before he begins to speak.**

I always made a conscious effort to use, over and over again, words which I knew Vanessa did not know, because I felt she could only learn new words and concept language by hearing them over and over again. For example, at first I would say, "Daddy's going bye-bye . . . bye, bye, Daddy . . . Daddy's all gone." As soon as I felt she understood these, I would say, "Daddy's going bye-bye to work; Daddy has to go to work; Daddy goes to work in the car." Then during the day I would ask her several times, "Where's Daddy?" She never answered, so I would answer the question myself and say, "Daddy's at work . . . Daddy

VANESSA'S AUDIOGRAM

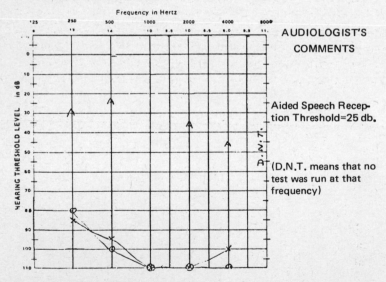

AUDIOLOGIST'S COMMENTS

Aided Speech Reception Threshold=25 db.

(D.N.T. means that no test was run at that frequency)

Vanessa shows a profound loss. However, with her aid she can now recognize speech at 25 dbs. Her response to aided pure tones is also extremely good.

went to work in the car . . . Daddy's working." I did this for many months and finally one day when I said "Where's Daddy? she said "Dada wook." As soon as she said that I said "Yes, Daddy's working at the office . . . Daddy works at the office everyday." I knew she had no idea what the words "office" and "everyday" meant, but I knew that if I didn't use these words she would never learn what they meant. Eventually she was saying "Dada wook office" without really having seen his office and without understanding what it meant. **All children as they learn language, use words without knowing what they mean.** Finally, I took her to Daddy's office, she saw him working there and she understood.

I did the same thing in many other situations. Once she understood "bye bye" I never said "Mommy's going bye bye." Instead I would say "Mommy's going shopping to buy ice cream" or "Mommy's going to a meeting" or "Mommy's going to the doctor" or "Mommy and Daddy are going to a party", or whatever. I knew perfectly well she didn't understand such words as "meeting", "party", or "shopping". However, because I used this language over and over and because of her own experiences, she eventually came to understand all of these words. Now, she has just turned five, and if I say "I'm going to a meeting", she replies with "Who's going to be there? Will Matthew's Mommy be there? What are you going to talk about?".

I found it very exciting to watch Vanessa's language grow in this manner. It seemed that if I used a word, phrase or expression often enough she would eventually use it correctly herself. When she was about three and a half, I began to post a short list of idioms or figures of speech that I would concentrate on using over the next two to three weeks as often as possible with her so that she would learn them. These were expressions which were very difficult to teach in lessons. I posted lists of these in the bathroom and on the kitchen wall so that my husband, babysitters, and anyone else who visited for any length of time could use them too. These lists were short—four or five expressions—so that everyone could remember them.

Expressions such as "Hurry up", "Not now", "In a little while", "I'm tired", "Do you know what?" appeared on an early list. Some of our current ones are "I don't believe it!", "Stop horsing around!", "You're putting me on", "That was a close call", "I'm all mixed up", "What a mystery!" "It slipped my mind", "You're pulling my leg".

I always tried to talk about things before they happened. At first, it was simply something like "Vanessa, later we're going bye bye . . . Mommy and Vanessa will go bye bye later . . . We'll go in the car." Once she learned "bye bye" she of course wanted to go immediately and would scream and carry on because we weren't going. But I would just say "No, not now, later . . . we'll go bye bye later". If I knew that we would be doing something the next day, I would say "Tomorrow we're going bye bye to Gammy's house". Again she would scream and carry on, but I would just keep repeating "No, tomorrow . . . we'll go to Gammy's house tomorrow". Sometimes, I'd feel like not telling her that things were going to happen just to avoid all the screaming and carrying on. However, I usually did, knowing that unless I did she would never learn the meanings of all the words and expressions associated with time and the passing of time—"not now", "later", "to-night", "this afternoon", "next week", "in two days", "next summer", "when you're eight years old". She told me today, "When I grow up first I want to be a teacher and then I want to be the tooth fairy". "When I grow up" is another expression I had on my list of idioms and now she understands and uses it appropriately.

Vanessa's speech is not completely intelligible to every-one at this time, but people who see her often can under-stand most of what she says. Her teacher feels that her speech is very good and has assured us that it will improve more with time. My husband and I have no problem understanding her and she comprehends almost everything we say. While I become concerned about her speech from time to time, I don't do much about it in a formal way because I feel that some day, she herself will become motivated to improve her own speech and to talk as well as everyone else.

Since the age of two and a half, Vanessa has attended regular schools with normally hearing children. I'll never forget her first day at nursery school. Hearing the chatter and questions of the other children really depressed me because Vanessa at this time was just beginning to put words together to form simple two and three word sentences. She talked only to my husband and me and her speech was such that only my husband and I could understand her. However, we were fortunate, because the teachers did essentially what we did at home—they talked to her anyway, whether she answered or not. And the teachers were just as thrilled as we were when, after several months of silence, she finally began to talk to them. I'll never forget my excitement when the school supervisor, who had said, "Good morning Vanessa. How are you today?", every day for five months with no response, telephoned me to say "Mrs. Vaughan—Vanessa said 'morning' to me today! Isn't that wonderful?"

In reading over what I have written, it seems so easy. But in all frankness, it wasn't easy! The first two years especially were emotionally and physically exhausting much of the time and very time-consuming with lesson preparations, trips to the library for just the right book, arranging for Vanessa to play with hearing children, planning special excursions, as well as all the time spent just talking and explaining the world to her . There were many days when I felt I couldn't cope another day, and there were many nights when I'd wake up and just cry at the reality of Vanessa's deafness, probably just because I was so tired.

However, everything became easier and easier as Vanessa's language grew. All the effort was and still is more than worthwhile and we are constantly rewarded, in fact overjoyed. One of my most rewarding times now is when she says "Mommy let's talk about something" and she'll go on "Let's talk about long ago when you were a little girl" or "Let's talk about me when I was a baby . . . Which was my bedroom? . . . Did I cry? . . . Who was my babysitter?" and on and on. Or when she says things like "Mommy, when I'm 15, can I fly to the moon?" Three and a half years ago, I thought such conversations would never be possible. So when she now asks "Can I fly to the moon?" as she did just a few days ago, I have to reply "Possibly."

Richard

*Richard is now five-and-a-half years old. He
tests as "profoundly deaf" in both ears. At the age
of two-and-a-half Richard began attending a regular
nursery school and is now in Kindergarten with normally hearing children. He gets along well with his
classmates and, in fact, was recently invited to
spend the weekend at the home of one of them. Richard
has a seven year old brother and a two-and-a-half year
old sister both with normal hearing. His mother is
not employed outside the home. In spite of
repeated ear infections and respiratory ill-
nesses Richard has made remarkable progress
in the auditory training program.*

Our son Richard was diagnosed as being severely deaf in
one ear and profoundly deaf in the other at the age of 14
months. Immediately, he began to wear a hearing aid.
Two-and-a-half years later more accurate tests revealed
that he was profoundly deaf in both ears, at which time
more powerful hearing aids were prescribed for each ear.

The first few months after the diagnosis of Richard's
deafness were very trying to say the least. The emotional
shock to me was so great that I became severely depressed.
It took several months of intense inner struggle and soul
searching before I was able to accept his handicap.

Two weeks after the diagnosis, we were introduced to
the Auditory Training teacher at the Hospital for Sick
Children who briefly explained that the hearing impaired
children who learn to use their residual hearing acquire
better speech than those who do not, and since Richard
had some hearing our aim would be to help him learn 'how
to listen'. **We were warned not to expect immediate
results.** A baby with normal hearing listens for about a
year before he starts vocalizing meaningfully. Richard had
been deprived of sound for 14 months and it might take a

17

while before he would start his first attempts at speech. We were told Richard would have to be 'bathed in sound' throughout his waking hours. We were to talk close to his hearing aid as much as possible, stressing certain simple sounds.

Richard did not like physical contact and preferred to play alone with a lot of space around him. This made it difficult to speak close to his aid, so I had to make the most of the situations where I could be close to him. Not being very talkative myself, I also found it difficult to talk to Richard, especially since I was not certain he could hear me—for the first few months that Richard wore his aid, we did not have any indication that it had helped him in any way. With some practice I found that if I asked myself "What can I say to him now?" there was always a great deal I could find to say. At mealtime, for example, I would sit beside his highchair and try to talk about all that was transpiring before him: "The soup's too hot, oh! . . . It's very hot! . . . Let's blow on it to cool it off . . . Blow, blow like this . . . Can you blow? . . . Oh! oh! we spilled some . . . Where's the kleenex? . . . There is the kleenex! . . . Let's wipe it off . . . Wipe, wipe, wipe like this . . . Can you wipe it off? . . . Good boy! . . . Now the table is clean and dry . . . The kleenex is wet . . . Touch it—it's wet . . . I'll throw it in the garbage".

When dressing or undressing him I'd talk about what we were doing. "Take off your right shoe . . . Take off your left shoe . . . Put your shoes beside your crib . . . Now let's take off your socks—one sock off, the other sock off . . . Let's put them in the hamper . . . Let's go find the hamper . . . There it is! It's in the washroom. Mommy will open the hamper and Richard will drop the socks in."

In other words, I simply talked to Richard about everything we did. **I tried to speak in a normal tone of voice pronouncing words clearly but without exaggeration,** varying the pitch of my voice to make it more interesting. It helped to imagine that he heard everything I said. The habit of constantly talking did not come naturally to me for a long time. It was frustrating not to get any response from him and even more so not to know how much of it he heard. It was tempting to slip into silence (which I did from time to time when I really got tired of talking) and it took a conscious effort not to do so.

When we started our weekly auditory training lessons at the Hospital (a few months after Richard's second birthday) we were introduced to the simple sounds associated with animals: "quack quack", "bow wow", "peep peep" etc. It took seven months before Richard could discriminate them auditorily and reproduce them with reasonable clarity.

With some experimentation I found that the most suitable and effective method for Richard and me was a formal lesson given at a regular time every day of the week. Initially, our lessons lasted only fifteen minutes. Gradually they extended to one hour, and later to an hour and a half. Boredom was one of the greatest foes during the first seven months. In order to keep his interest in lessons alive, I tried to change the material as often as I could, as well as changing the method of presenting the same words.

During the time that Richard was particularly reluctant to have his lessons I used reward as a means of getting his attention. At the end of the lesson I would reward him with an inexpensive (10 to 15 cent) plastic toy purchased at the novelty section of a department or grocery store. This, in itself, was an opportunity to introduce new vocabulary. If I had a plastic motorcycle for him, we could talk about its color, its wheels, the noise it makes. If it was a whistle, we could blow it and listen to the sound it made. If it was a ball, we could throw it, bounce it, roll it and catch it.

Sometime at the beginning of his second year in auditory training I introduced the expression, "It's all finished", and as soon as he understood its meaning I started to use an alarm clock with the alarm set for the duration of the lesson. As soon as the alarm went off, I would immediately stop the lesson, explaining "The alarm went off. We are all finished for today." This solved the problem of his getting up in the middle of the lesson saying, "No more."

As the habit of lessons became established and I could rely more and more on pictures, books and games, the need for ploys such as the alarm clock and rewards disappeared.

Richard's learning did not stop at lessons. **Reinforcement of the lesson material and acquisition of other new language went on on a casual basis throughout the day.** During meals the toy chick would be eating with Richard: "The chick that says peep peep is eating some bread, peep peep. Oh! Oh! Where's the chick that says peep peep? . . . It's under the cup! . . . Peep peep!" At bedtime we said "bye bye" to the bus that goes "bu bu bu", and the chick that goes "peep peep", and the dog that goes "bow wow", etc. On our car trips we brought along toy buses, cars, trains, boats, motorcycles, dolls and farm animals. When we were passing a bus we could point to the toy bus and then the bus we were passing saying: "The bus goes bu bu bu". On the trips to the country, we'd stop the car if we saw some farm animals grazing, point them out and identify them.

Interest has always been a very important factor in Richard's learning. If he is interested he learns much more quickly than when he is not; if he is not interested it may take months to learn one word or one concept. Numbers illustrate this well. We tried to count rocks, candies, cars, flowers and a long list of other objects, but none kept his interest long enough to count to five until I introduced money. I bought him a piggy bank and if he gave me the right amount of pennies he was allowed to keep them. Within two weeks he was counting to 14 and his interest in numbers has not died since.

He also learns more quickly in situations and activities

that he finds enjoyable. Being an active, sports-minded child he prefers any kind of an action game to a sitting down lesson, especially if other members of the family can participate. When he was learning prepositions I made an obstacle course of furniture and ropes. We crawled, jumped and hid "under", "over", "behind", "in", "beside", everything in the house. This he enjoyed tremendously and learned relatively quickly. In order to teach him the verb "to land" I learned to fold paper airplanes and the whole family had hours of fun throwing their airplanes and watching where they "landed". Ball games of all sorts have been a good source of important vocabulary. They have been especially useful at times when Richard was too sick to have a sit down lesson. There is a great opportunity for repetition: *throw the ball; catch the ball; roll the ball; I caught it; I missed it; I dropped it; hit the ball; kick the ball; it's lost; let's find it; too low; too high; let's take turns; etc.*

When Richard was two-and-a-half years old he became ill with pneumonia. This was a setback in itself but more serious was the resulting ill health that has plagued him ever since. A week after his return from the hospital Richard had his first ear infection. From this point on he has had recurring ear and chest infections with the resulting middle ear fluid build-up. The years when he was on monaural amplification were especially difficult. At one time he went for two months without being able to wear his hearing aid. When he was finally able to wear it I was shocked to find out that he had forgotten how to listen. For two years I lived in constant fear that someone was going to tell me that he would not be able to benefit from Auditory Training. It is fortunate that Richard now has binaural amplifcation; when one ear is infected, the other usually is not, so we can still carry on with the Auditory Training without experiencing setbacks.

With the onset of ill-health came behavior problems. They were aggravated by my third pregnancy. As Richard grew older he became increasingly frustrated because of lack of adequate language. I believe that my changing appearance and my inability to pick him up as often as he was accustomed to made him even more resentful and angry. He wanted to assert his authority in every situation. At bedtime, for example, he would resist putting on his pyjamas; if he was left with his clothes on he kicked the door and screamed until someone came in. If an attempt was made to undress him the same struggle occurred. It seemed that no matter what course of action was taken he would find something to protest against. He became aggressive with his peers—the neighborhood children were constantly complaining and I became a nervous wreck. Everytime I heard a child crying I ran outside to see if it was Richard hurting someone. I tried everything I could think of to get through to him: showing more affection, talking, and in the end, punishing him. Isolating him from the other children was effective if I could make him stay in his room. We were forced to put a lock on his bedroom door. We were watchful for signs of co-operation on his part: whenever he stopped kicking the door I would

RICHARD'S AUDIOGRAM

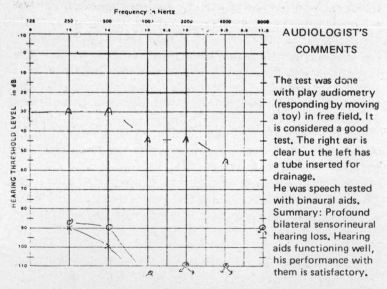

AUDIOLOGIST'S
COMMENTS

The test was done with play audiometry (responding by moving a toy) in free field. It is considered a good test. The right ear is clear but the left has a tube inserted for drainage.
He was speech tested with binaural aids.
Summary: Profound bilateral sensorineural hearing loss. Hearing aids functioning well, his performance with them is satisfactory.

Richard shows profound loss especially in the high frequencies. With aids he perceives speech through the speech range. He has problems with ear infections.

immediately open it, take him in my arms and explain once again why he was being punished.

Towards his fourth birthday we began to notice a marked improvement in his behavior. His vocabulary had increased a great deal by then and he was able to understand verbally the consequences of his bad behavior. Praise became meaningful to him now and was a very useful tool in solving many problems. If he asked a child for a toy rather than snatching it away I praised him and explained that if he did that more often they would let him play with their toys and would allow him to participate in their games. As soon as he saw the effect that his improved manners had on the other children his aggressive behavior disappeared almost completely.

In the first two years I taught Richard everything he knew. It was easy to understand him since I knew exactly how he was saying the words he knew. When he started to pick up vocabulary on his own and to put the words together I began having more and more trouble understanding him. It was especially distressing when he was trying to tell me something about school. At this time I approached Richard's teacher and asked her to write a brief note every day informing me of the main activities of the day. Knowing what Richard was trying to tell me I could help him to express himself in a proper form. For example, if I got from Richard: "Richard ... school ... under the bridge ... over the bridge ... car" and the note said, "Richard was playing in the block centre today", I could restate his story in a proper form, "Oh yes! Richard was playing with the blocks at school today. Richard built a bridge and made the car go over the bridge and under the bridge." This also made him feel that he was successful at communicating his message and encouraged him to talk more.

I have always tried to organize my day in such a way that the rest of the family would not suffer because of the time I had to spend with Richard. Our older son, Tommy, is only one-and-a-half years older than Richard and being

23

quite young too, he needed my attention and expressed resentment when I spent time with Richard. After a certain amount of conflict we were able to arrive at a compromise solution; during the lesson Tommy would play quietly if he knew he would be allowed to stay up for half an hour after Richard's bedtime so I could spend time with him doing things he enjoyed doing. Now that he is older the nature of our activities has changed but I still try to spend time with him alone if he wants it.

When Richard was two-and-a-half years old, our third child was born. For the first year of Lucie's life the time and duration of Richard's lessons depended entirely on the time and the duration of her naps. By the time she was one year old her naps became so erratic that I had to find a neighbor to take care of her for two hours every morning so I could work with Richard. As soon as she was old enough, Lucie also insisted on having her "lesson". I still spend some time with her every afternoon reading, drawing, doing puzzles or singing.

I try to resist the temptation to talk only about Richard when the whole family is present. Our favorite topic of conversation at dinnertime is: "What did you do today?" All the children take turns telling what they did during the day. This turned out to be very helpful in encouraging Richard to talk about his experiences.

Richard has been in the Auditory Training program for three-and-a-half years now. After he mastered the first basic sounds his progress became more rapid. Daily lessons are still very much a part of our life. His facility in acquiring speech becomes greater as his vocabulary increases.

At the age of two years, Richard's vocabulary was barely seven words, at the age of three he had about 200 and at the age of four years he had about 500. Now he is five years old and I have lost count of his vocabulary. He has picked up a lot of words and expressions on his own. He makes a very good attempt to communicate in sentences and while his speech may not be entirely comprehensible to a stranger, his friends and family members have little difficulty understanding him. We do not have more behavioral problems with Richard than with our other two children, who are normal in every respect.

Richard now attends kindergarten with normally hearing children. He gets along well with his classmates; in fact, he was recently invited to spend the weekend at the home of one of them. We are very proud of him.

Someone once asked me, if I had an opportunity to take Richard to an Auditory Training teacher more frequently and thus be absolved of all the responsibility for lessons, would I take it? In all honesty I said "no" for several reasons. The most important is that most of Richard's learning occurs on a casual basis when lesson material is constantly reinforced and new language is introduced. Being his teacher I know what he knows and what he needs to learn and can provide him with the language he needs at the time he needs it. Another reason is that the daily lessons and the constant interaction with Richard resulted in a deep communication between Richard and me even before he could communicate verbally. He has always had the security of knowing that even if no one else understood him, I did.

Peter

Peter is two-and-a-half years old and is an only child. When he becomes three, he will attend a nursery school with hearing children. His mother is not employed outside the home. Since English is not her mother tongue, she felt initially that she did not have the training and ability to teach her child. However, Peter has been doing extremely well in the auditory training program and his mother is becoming much more confident about her ability to use and to teach him English.

Peter's hearing impairment had been suspected by his pediatrician when he was two months old. Nevertheless, Peter did not receive his hearing aid until the day before his first birthday. Although we lived in doubt for several months, we were shocked with the diagnosis of deafness. I took it hard and I lost my desire to live. The fact that we were in a new city with no friends and relatives and the fact that I am a person who doesn't express her feelings or thoughts didn't help at that time.

I have always felt responsible for Peter's hearing impairment especially in the beginning. The cause of Peter's impairment is said to be of a hereditary or unknown reason. By not knowing what really caused his hearing loss I find myself wondering "What did I do wrong?"

But my emotional turmoil was somehow settled by my decision to devote my whole life if needed so that Peter would reach his potential regardless of his handicap. Peter is our first and only child and I always had confidence in his capabilities. **Even if he didn't have any hearing for a year he did not lose his intelligence!** I even felt that he was more alert, curious and observant.

Not knowing anything about deafness, its degrees and

implications and having a child who has just been diagnosed "from severely to profoundly hard of hearing" is an
emotional shock and a chaotic situation. It is like not
knowing what to ask and from whom to ask it and what is
the priority.

I feel that we were fortunate to be in the right place at
the right time. The teacher from the Hospital for Sick
Children got in touch with us in a matter of days and we
started Peter with the auditory approach. Since we wanted
Peter to be a normal person the auditory approach was just
what we needed.

My first problem was to get Peter wearing his hearing
aid all the time. When he first heard a voice through his
hearing aid he got scared and cried and removed the
earmould. For the first weeks, if not a month, he kept on
removing the earmould all the time. Sometimes 50 times a
day. I always kept on putting it right back without
showing any emotion or saying anything, which is hard to
do. I also found that it helped by switching it to the other
ear. I had realized that as long as I kept his eyes and hands
busy he would not touch his hearing aid. So, I kept him
occupied all the time to the extent that I never did any
housework while he was awake. At that time I was having
as many as three lessons a day which was a tiring
experience. Peter would throw the miniature animals on
the floor and I would calmly pick them up (telling him
that he was naughty) and put them on the table with the
result of having them thrown in a second. When he was
older I would slap his hand and after that I would just
warn him about getting his hand slapped. The other
problem was that he wouldn't let something go. I solved
that problem by showing him or telling him what was
about to come. Of course, there are certain objects that I
just can't use in a lesson because he is just not going to give
them up.

Up to now, I haven't a set time for a lesson. Peter loves
his lessons and asks me for one. We do have a lesson as soon
as he asks me or when I am in my best form. **My mood**

definitely reflects on the success of the lesson. When I enjoy the lesson he enjoys it too. If I am in a hurry or in a bad mood, the lesson ends up in failure and a lot of tension. Children get bored too, so I never say something many times. I usually repeat something later on.

When Peter was a baby, in order to teach him the animal sounds I would have the animals shown to him while he was being fed. I would let him handle them while he was eating. The wall next to him had some pictures of animals and later on colored cars and airplanes. His room has big pictures all around and several times a day I would ask him where was the "meow" or the "quack quack" and later on "cat" and "duck" and so on. Of course, I showed him the real animals and Peter reacted as if they were his long lost brothers. He would run to catch them and hug them while imitating the sounds they make and really being happy.

I am always spending a lot of time looking for books. At first I was trying to get colored picture books. Later on a good clear drawing was sufficient. I have always been reading a lot of books to Peter. I would ask him if he wanted another book and I would keep on reading. I always have some books within his reach and some for the lesson only. Now the way things are he is after me all day long telling me "Read me a book". When I ask him which one he wants he is able to tell me the title. He really listens to what I am reading since one day I started reading a page the way it was printed and therefore with words that he did not know. He started screaming and turned around very upset telling me off. I repeated the same thing later on and although I was coloring my voice as much as possible I had the same reactions from Peter. Sometimes I read to him ten books in a row. Lately I see that he is picking up sentences and new words from the books.

Of course our lives have changed. I don't make schedules and plans anymore. I don't cook or bake and I am not a tidy housekeeper any longer. Peter is the centre of my attention. I never felt that I was giving up too much since I love Peter very much and since we have a goal to achieve.

At first it seemed like I was just giving or putting in all my time and efforts and getting nothing in return. Actually I was expecting too much too soon. The airplane sound was achieved almost immediately and after two months of lessons every day two to three times a day he would respond to 13 words. At that time he wasn't saying much at all, not any consonants any way. In a period of two-and-a-half months since he started wearing his hearing aid he first used consonants in his babbling. After four months, Peter began to wear binaural aids and has worn these ever since.

Now that I am getting results out of my hard work it just seems easier to keep on going. I believe that everything is a habit and even the hardest task that you undertake after a period of time becomes a way of life.

PETER'S AUDIOGRAM

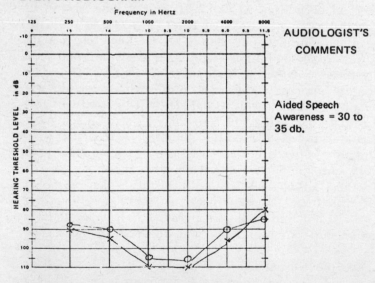

Peter shows a profound loss. The audiologist was only able to make an estimate of Speech Awareness when he is wearing his aids.

In the beginning I was terrified that I had to teach Peter a language that wasn't my native tongue, but then I decided to take a step at a time and go from week to week. I could handle Peter the first year and I can handle him now. In the future who knows? Maybe my husband will have to do the job, maybe he will need a tutor. Maybe by that time my English is going to be adequate. I am learning too, for one thing, to have more freedom with the language.

I feel that what really made Peter so talkative was the fact that all day long I was talking about every single experience that was happening and I was verbalizing every single action. After a while it seems very natural to say "Now I am putting two spoons of sugar in my tea and I am stirring it with the spoon."

I always color my voice and do talk louder. At no time do I encourage lipreading and Peter is not lipreading.

Training Peter to notice the different sounds and associating their meaning wasn't easy and we are still working on it. I had started blaming myself for Peter's inability to identify different sounds, but like most of the time, I got results unexpectedly. He first heard a noise from upstairs and he was terrified. I spent half an hour drawing something like our apartment building with people in each square. Ever since he always hears the noises from upstairs although most of the time they are not loud. Now he can also hear a big truck passing although we are on the 14th floor. He can hear the blender and the mixer and somebody knocking at our door. As well as a cup being set on the table or a toy being moved and so on. I found out that it really helps in training his auditory ability by not having the radio or TV on. Sometimes he can identify different sounds. As soon as Peter hears a sound I take him and show him the source of the sound.

If Peter is watching TV and I want to explain to him what he is seeing, I just go over to his hearing aid and tell him so that I surpass the noise level.

While Peter is awake I never see him or consider him as being a handicapped or deaf child. I should admit though that while he wasn't near me and especially for the first months I kept saying to myself "My child is deaf, but he is going to overcome his deafness." I don't like the words deaf or handicapped and I don't use them, but people do.

Somehow I am pleased that I got used to the sound of the word "deaf" so the day that a lady asked me if I was the mother of the deaf child, I just smiled and said "yes". I had to become stronger because since we live with all sorts of people you might even meet some who think deafness is an infectious disease.

Peter is 27 months old now. I would describe him as being a happy, friendly, affectionate and nothing-escapes-my-attention kind of little child. He talks all day long. He is the boy that has his face glued to the car or bus window and does not stop for a minute verbalizing everything that he sees—from the "big red truck" to the "smoke coming out of the chimney". I am always ready to add "Oh yes, Peter, it's a very big red truck and did you see? It has very big wheels too."

Peter is making little sentences and he knows 585 words. His speech is comparatively clear and people seem to be very impressed.

My motto with Peter has been "Reach what you can't".

Matthew

*Matthew is now six-and-a-half years old and
is in Grade 1 at his local public school where he
is doing well. Matthew has a four-and-a-half year
old brother. His mother is not employed outside
the home. Matthew tests as being "severely
deaf". However, after six years of auditory
training he responds as a hard-of-hearing
child when he is wearing his aids.*

Matthew's hearing loss was suspected at the age of six
weeks and confirmed by an Ear, Nose and Throat specialist
at two months. For a long time the extent of the loss was
difficult to ascertain since he sometimes appeared to hear
sounds which at other times aroused no response in him.
He was fitted with a hearing aid at eight months and wore
it in one ear until he was 14 months old. At that time it
was removed because his doctor felt he probably was
aphasic rather than hearing impaired. When he was about
28 months old he was again fitted with a hearing aid and
he has continued to wear one since then. Shortly after this
he began using a Y cord (a single aid with a cord to each
ear), and when he was four-and-a-half years old he got
binaural aids.

Immediately following the initial diagnosis (at two
months) I was in contact with a teacher of hearing
impaired children at the Hospital for Sick Children and she
advised me to talk loudly near his ear. This I did while
seating him on my lap facing away from me. I also sang to
him a great deal, making up silly songs and changing the
pitch of my voice to relieve the tedium. The first awareness of sound that I noticed came when I had been doing
this for about six months. Matthew smiled when I changed
my voice while singing "Baa Baa Black Sheep". Otherwise
he showed little or no reaction to sound, though he did
baffle us occasionally with a response that was unexpected.

When he was 20 months old we began to see the

teacher once a week. She had agreed to take him on a diagnostic or evaluative basis as there was still some question of his being aphasic rather than hearing impaired. I had obtained material on working with aphasics, and had discussed this with speech therapists so I knew that our approach with the teacher was much the same as that which might have been prescribed for aphasics. Therefore there was no concern about our causing him further difficulties by so working with him. When we first began formal lessons we felt that Matthew had no speech comprehension. We talked loudly near his ear and he began to respond to his lessons very soon after we started.

The summer prior to his starting nursery school he seemed to progress very little. He did not want to sit down to work, so we did very little in a formal way. He said "No" all the time and seemed to have forgotten all he knew. However, he soon demonstrated that he had not done so, and that he'd simply been storing information. I took him to the local public school where they had a "play school". He appeared not to hear or understand most of what was going on around him. However, later he'd sit at home and seemed to be trying to "sing" Old MacDonald Had A Farm (a playschool favorite). His rendition only vaguely resembled the original but there was an unmistakable kernel present. During all this time we always spoke to him in full sentences and tried to expand his vocabulary. For example, he knew the words "duck" and "water" so we'd say "Let's go upstairs and have a bath with the duck and water", until we finally dropped the known words and he understood what we meant. He often used phrases "Where is it?" and "What is it?", both of which we'd used constantly with him in lessons.

When he began nursery school at age three, he had a vocabulary of about 40 to 60 words, most of which would be incomprehensible to anyone but me. We asked that his teacher treat him as any other member of the class. (This we have requested from all his teachers, playschool supervisors, etc. He has always gone to a normal school and is presently in Grade 1 in the local public school). He talked very little initially and the teacher was concerned about making him sit and listen to stories when he could grasp so little. However, I helped her to understand that if he were to be allowed to wander off then, he would likely not be interested in participating later when he might have a larger language base. He tried to appropriately use what language he had as can be demonstrated with the following:— When he was just over three years he came running to me one day shouting "Mommy, mommy, Matthew spilled mouth". At that time he did not have the language for "vomiting" but he, nevertheless, expressed the situation vividly. His auditory facility also increased that year. He had previously been unable to hear the telephone ring even when standing beside it with his aids on, and now he was able to tell me when it rang in the next room. His teacher also learned to sit him on her lap facing away from her when she spoke to him. I always sat beside or slightly behind him when working with him and I'm sure he thought I had an unbelievably itchy nose since I frequently seemed to be scratching it when I spoke to him as he faced me. I developed this habit early on as it seemed more natural than overtly covering my mouth. I also had him eating in the breakfast nook while I busied myself in the kitchen and spoke loudly to him from there. Another habit I got into was to repeat after him what he had said. This confirmed that I had understood him and also gave him another reinforcement of the correct sentence pattern and pronunciation.

Repetition has remained a most important facet of Matthew's learning experience. When he was younger I would introduce new pictures by first stating what they were, then laying three, or four, or five pictures down, again repeating what they represented while pointing to each one. Then I would ask him to give them to me one at a time (always using full sentences). If he could not, I would say "Here it is, here is the . . .," then I would repeat the name of each object again as I put it away. I always mixed known material in with the new so that he would get positive reinforcement several times during the lesson. When looking for pictures, I would often come across something he knew or that I thought he knew and I would include it with the material the teacher had given me. I still follow this procedure, and also work with him on words she has used that I do not think he knows though these words are not on the vocabulary list she gives me.

Our main focus from the beginning was on his ability to comprehend language rather than on his speech. We lavishly praised his every effort and his self image is very positive. His speech has greatly improved over the last couple of years and we now correct his pronunciation, without making a big issue of it. Matthew understands that he cannot hear without his hearing aids and that his ears "don't work" very well. He sometimes asks why, and also wonders if he can stop wearing his aids when he grows older since he is now "learning to hear". He has always

MATTHEW'S AUDIOGRAM

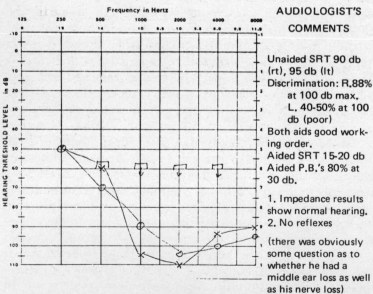

AUDIOLOGIST'S COMMENTS

Unaided SRT 90 db (rt), 95 db (lt)
Discrimination: R.88% at 100 db max.
L. 40-50% at 100 db (poor)
Both aids good working order.
Aided SRT 15-20 db
Aided P.B.'s 80% at 30 db.

1. Impedance results show normal hearing.
2. No reflexes

(there was obviously some question as to whether he had a middle ear loss as well as his nerve loss)

Matthew has a very severe loss but is able to recognize quite a lot of speech without his aid providing it is very loud. With his aid he recognizes around 80% at 30 dbs and some much less loudly.

been outgoing and I have never seen him avoid a situation because he felt self-conscious about his hearing loss. He began using phrases and simple sentences when he was four and has progressed to using fairly complicated sentences as a matter of course.

From the beginning we always had faith that auditory training would be helpful to, and even successful for Matthew. No one ever gave us any guarantees that this would be so, but we operated on this assumption. This positive outlook undoubtedly was conveyed to him. We took pride in his attempts to learn and tried not to make too many comparisons with his peers. It would be false to say that we never were worried, or depressed, or fed up, but we always seemed to come through, often with the support of other parents in the same situation. I tried to work with him every day, and found it much easier to do so once he started responding more readily. It is a lot easier to keep putting something in when you are getting some feedback. Matthew was not always co-operative and lessons were sometimes very trying for both of us. For example, when he was three years old, I used Smarties to induce him to do his work. These were effective not only for their taste appeal but also because they served to make him more aware of colors. I would give him one or two at the end of each segment of the lesson, gradually weaning him to a couple at the end, and finally to none at all. To this day he frequently does not get his dessert (which we refer to as a treat) until after his lesson. When he was five he frequently would begin a lesson by a long tirade, "This takes too long . . . I'm too tired . . . It's too hard for me . . . etc." I gradually learned to accept this and quietly told him that I was sorry he was so tired and if this were so he really should go to bed. This usually toned down the situation and the lesson could progress.

I really disliked tracking down pictures in magazines, etc. so I would often draw a picture. My drawings were terrible, but he got the point, and how else could I produce a fall picture with colored leaves, acorns, a food stand, ripe and green apples, pumpkins, a stream, etc. etc.

My main source of material was the *Cat in the Hat* dictionary. I bought two, cut them up, and placed the pictures in alphabetical order in envelopes. I could usually find a picture for about six out of the ten subjects I wanted.

This year we can do most of our teaching by giving verbal definitions. Besides making it easier to plan it is also nice to realize that your child's vocabulary has expanded to such a degree. We use stories to illustrate vocabulary and Matthew loves that. For example, "A little girl was playing outside and saw a boy fall down and hurt himself. She went over to him and helped him get up and was nice to him. Do you think her mother would *approve* or *disapprove* of what she did?" He prefers that I tell the stories, but will also make up a few himself. It is a pleasant way of conveying new information. We still illustrate some words with physical action and this is also very popular. He is sometimes asked to complete a story for which he has been given the first sentence. His story is printed and he is helped to read it. He greatly enjoys this procedure.

I make an effort to post in the kitchen a list of the words or ideas we are working on that week. This helps to remind me to reinforce them and also lets my husband know what he might talk about. Occasionally, I remember to write down for further lessons words which crop up that he does not know.

Often when he digresses and wants to know about something else during a lesson, I try to give him the information. When he uses this to avoid his work, I let him know that the lesson must come first.

Singing has played a large role in my work with Matthew. I sing almost as badly as I draw, but once again he is amused by it and learns from it. If he is having trouble with a word, I will frequently start singing it in a silly voice and he tries to imitate me. He likes to sing and is picking up songs at school. He tends not to sing much there, and we finally realized that this was because he would not be able to hear the words if he were trying to sing at the same time as the other children. (We now do some whispering in our lessons. Though he has some difficulty hearing a whisper, he is improving and can at times pick out individual words from among eight or nine rhyming words).

We wanted Matthew to be a normal person coping with a disability. In order to do this we had to treat him as normally as possible all the while teaching him language and increasing his auditory skills. This has become increasingly easier as his skills improve. Had we treated him differently and made a lot of exceptions when he was younger, we would undoubtedly have had a great deal of difficulty getting him to behave in a socially acceptable manner at a later stage.

We are endlessly delighted with the progress he has made, and are particularly pleased to see him relate to us and his peers in the same manner as any other six year old boy would.

John

*John is now four-and-a-half years old and attends
Junior Kindergarten in his local public school.
Each afternoon he goes to a day care nursery until
his mother returns from work. John's teacher feels
that he gets along well with his classmates. John
is an only child. His mother works full time
and has done so since John was four months
old. John has been wearing two hearing aids
since he was three-and-a-half and this is
still in its experimental stage. He tests
as being "profoundly deaf".*

It was September, 1970, that John our only child came
into our lives. He appeared to be a happy normal baby. In
retrospect, he didn't give us much reason to believe otherwise except that he didn't make the babbling sounds of the
normal infant. He never pulled the little knob on his blue
jay to hear the prayer from Hansel and Gretel. He was
visually very alert.

About a year after we first suspected something was
wrong and after seeing many specialists and completing
many tests we were told that John was profoundly deaf.
John was 20 months old at this time.

It was the end of May. He was fitted with an earmould
and a hearing aid was loaned to us for the summer. We were
asked to return in three months time to assess his response
with the hearing aid.

When we were given the hearing aid, we expected to be
told how much response we might get from John. After
all, these people looked after people with hearing aids
every day. **Looking back we can now appreciate why they
really can't tell any parent how much their child will hear
because every child is different and responds in his unique
way.**

In September of the same year we were introduced to

auditory training at the Hospital for Sick Children. We were told that this is one method of teaching deaf children, and that there were others. We were introduced to those as well. The doctor explained that in choosing this method of teaching John, we would be committed to giving lessons to our child ourselves and that the next few years would not be easy. While the teacher would offer a lesson plan and illustrate methods of teaching the child to listen, the mother would have to do most of the work at home.

The major decision for us at this time was not whether or not to choose auditory training; we knew this was what we wanted for John. However, I was, and still am, a full-time working mother and my job is not just nine to five; it does not end when I leave work but consumes what many people would consider to be free time. I leave for work before seven each morning. Many people thought I should give up my job when John's hearing loss was diagnosed, particularly since we chose to educate John solely by auditory training. But we had so many factors to consider.

I had already signed a contract to work for another year and we were saving to buy our own home—something we wanted for John very much. John had always been a happy child and I felt had been getting excellent and loving care from the woman who took care of him when I worked. My employer discussed John's problem and auditory training with me and was very understanding—she was willing to adjust my schedule so that I could take him to the hospital for his lesson every week and was willing to accommodate emergencies such as extra trips for broken aids, lost earmoulds, etc. Her understanding was very important in helping us decide that I would continue to work. Although I decided to keep on working, I was always prepared to quit immediately if I, or John's teacher, felt he was not progressing as he should. Since John has been doing very well, this has not been necessary.

Naturally, I have wished many times that I could be

home planning better lessons, but when I am home, the day goes by and I am not always as well organized. I have always felt that the quality of time I spend with John is more important than the quantity of time. And my husband and I devote ourselves fully to John after work and on the weekends.

John had been wearing his aid for about four months when we first started auditory training. The aid alone had brought no vocabulary or new sounds from him. We attended classes once a week and went over basic sounds that any normal child would have mastered by his age; "meow", "ah ———", "bow wow", "moo", "bu bu bu", "quack quack". My husband and I worked about thirty minutes twice a day and when we weren't doing lessons we talked continually. After seven weeks John spontaneously said "Meow", when he saw a pussy cat. Other sounds seemed to follow fairly rapidly. When I say rapidly, I mean about one sound per week. This response seemed a long time in coming, but when it did come it thrilled us and spurred us on.

It is difficult now to look back and remember each milestone in John's language and speech development; but each week we saw progress. Each week we worked on a few new words. He could not understand simple instructions for quite some time but with acquisition of more vocabulary he started to understand simple instructions about nine months after we started auditory training; for example, *Sit down, Say thank you, Be careful, Say good bye,* etc.

One incident that stands out in my mind is when John spilled milk or dropped a dish I would say "Oh, John" with some emphasis. One day I heard him in the bathroom saying something that sounded like "Oh-shawn". Soon I realized that he said this each time he or I did something like spilling something. I realized he was saying exactly what I said to him, "Oh John". In other words, he associated the words "Oh! John", with this kind of incident and not with his name. He was calling me "Muppy" by the spring of 1973, approximately six months after he commenced auditory training. I loved him for that name, even though it sounded like I was a worn out old dog.

John had a formal lesson for about thirty or forty minutes each day. We usually had lessons after our evening meal. We had an average of six lessons a week. At the first we taught sounds and words associated with objects. It was easy then to illustrate what was meant, but as time progressed, concepts and more abstract words were harder to present; for example, *angry, sad, pain, happy, tired, hungry, worried, beautiful.* You begin to realize that some words become long term words. You have no idea how many words in English have several meanings until you begin to teach language.

I did much of my teaching through drawing; for ex-

JOHN'S AUDIOGRAM

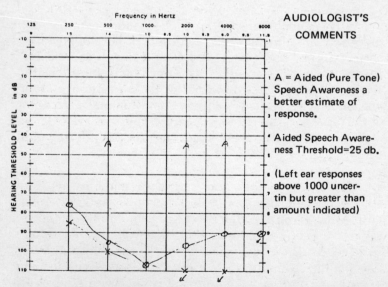

John's audiogram shows that he has a profound loss. He is making extremely good use of his aid to be aware of speech at 25 db. This differential is typical of the listening hearing impaired.

ample, *happy* and *sad faces, curly* and *straight hair, thick* and *thin crayons,* etc. I have also used many pictures from magazines, coloring books, catalogues and story books to illustrate lesson content. Trips in the car to family, friends, hospital and vacation are all used to reinforce language.

I don't always believe in interfering in a child's play to give a lesson, as I feel play is very important to the child and he or she needs some time to be alone to work through some of his own problems. Play can be used, however, when you are invited to share or see an opportunity to teach.

Because I worked, John began attending a day care nursery when he was two and a half. This exposed him to other normal children. Especially because we have no other children, this has been important for his overall development. The nursery does not have a sophisticated curriculum but the children do all the things that children like to do and are disciplined when they need it. They play in a large garden with sand, mud and water, they watch the lady who cares for them bake cookies, plant a garden, and do many other daily tasks.

When I get home from work I prepare supper and then devote nearly all of my time to John and his lesson. In the past year I have spent one evening a week planning all my lessons for the week. It was not easy thinking up four or five different ways to present a word but as time went on, I became more skillful and quite surprised at what I could think of.

I have always been very consistent with lesson time and it has become a habit. John now expects that he will have his lesson after supper, except on weekends when we usually want to get it over with early in the day so we can do something else together. I have occasionally invited another child to participate in our lessons when John has not wanted to stop playing and sit down because the other child was playing with him. As soon as he saw the other child enjoying it, John wanted to join in too. I have also used a teddy bear or favorite animal, doll or puppet when he has not wanted a lesson. I would just begin giving teddy the lesson and John was there almost instantly. As John acquired more language he would often be the teacher and this would be good for language development as well. I tried to involve my husband in lessons often because it helps to have a third person when the child has difficulty following instructions. For example, when trying to get John to answer the question "What's this?" I might ask Daddy first. The child hears his answer and then understands what is expected of him.

I always give John lots of praise as this encourages him. I remember when John first started to recognize sounds. His teacher would pat him on the head and say "good boy". John soon started patting himself on the head and saying "good boy".

One of the most frustrating times for me is when John gets undressed to bathe and his aid is removed. He often gets into mischief and I find it difficult to discipline him effectively at these times.

Quite often on weekends we try to give John other experiences such as shopping, car rides, family visits, Sunday school instead of formal lessons. When we visited a fair, we reviewed the names of farm animals, talked about where milk comes from, etc. even though this was not lesson content at the time. I always tried to make the most of every experience. Very often John will lead me into a lesson by bringing me an object or picture. **We talk about it right then and there when he is interested.** A great deal of his learning takes place in this way.

John occasionally gets quite fed up with lessons. There are days when he is tired and not prepared to listen but these times are few. We don't attend classes during July and August but continue to have more informal and less structured lessons. This is a good time to teach summer words; for example, *tent, seaside, sand, pail, stones, holidays, sea, lake, boat,* etc.

Six months after Auditory Training started John could hear the telephone and someone knocking at the door if there were not too many other distractions.

By the end of his first nine months we were given opposites such as *heavy* and *light, light* and *dark, big* and *little, hot* and *cold, fast* and *slow, open* and *close, loud* and *quiet, neat* and *messy,* etc. to teach. Verbs such as *buy, cook, drive, feed, fix, hide, hold, march, pat, wear* were words we were given to learn during the summer. Prepositions were stressed one at a time. For example, for a couple of weeks we worked on "on", then "behind" for the next couple of weeks, etc.

Major concepts such as what things are made of were presented one at a time, first *wood,* then *glass, metal, rubber, paper.* As an example, when teaching "made of paper", I used a paper cup, a paper envelope, a paper plate, a stamp, etc. Language for the parts of the house, clothing, body, were all presented in much the same manner. Christmas time, Easter, Spring, Autumn all brought new words and we presented them as they arose.

We try to review as much as possible but this is difficult when John's vocabulary has now expanded to a point where we have lost count of the number of words he uses. If you have time to try to keep a record of your child's progress. Record dates of those lessons or new words and concepts that are presented. John is now (age four) forming simple sentences and phrases; for example, "Where are we going?", "I no like cauliflower", "I'm not feeling very well", "I'm tired!", "You got a man?", "I go to your house another day", "My name is John". He spontaneously says "thank you" and "please", on most occasions.

It is difficult to monitor all the language that John has developed. He seems to advance in spurts. John's speech is quite clear to most people that are around him for any length of time. Most of the words he has been using are those which he has had lessons on. But recently he has begun to pick up and use words he hears casually. It is such a wonderful surprise to have him use words I know I haven't taught him.

John is now enrolled in a normal junior kindergarten. He has had no major problems that I am aware of. The teacher did comment that sometimes the other children get a little frustrated. He has been able to bring home notes and small pieces of information such as the policeman visited or that the teacher was ill. I explained very simply his hearing loss and his aid to his teacher. **I minimized any problems as these only put people on their guard and create anxiety for them.**

John has started wearing a second aid in his left ear. The hearing in his left ear is worse than his right ear so only time will tell whether a second aid will help.

When my husband and I embarked on auditory training, we accepted the fact we alone and no one else were responsible for John's education. We chose to commit ourselves fully to this method and do it as best we could. We do feel it would be extremely unfair to any child to change one's methods every time you hear a mother talk about what she does or does not do. People can really confuse you but they can also be of great assistance if you take all the advice and gear it to your child's and family's needs. **It is a slow steady grind and there are no magical tricks to suddenly give your child language.**

We happen to believe in prayer so we believe that we have been given strength to cope with each day. We have and still do work hard with John. There are no short cuts. We have, however, grown into it. Our lives have changed but not all for the worse. We have gained phenomenal insight from the experience of teaching and sharing with our child.

There are times when we have been grieved because John could not hear some very special music or enjoy the sound of the sea or when he has bumped himself because he could not hear us warn him fast enough. There are, however, countless precious times which are difficult to put in writing. The entire concept of auditory training is very exciting. Try to imagine the relationship you develop with this child who is depending on you to help him.

Part II

Auditory training

in lessons at home

a teacher's approach

through daily routines

through books

can include nursery school

Mother and Jonathan doing a lesson

Auditory training in lessons at home

Teaching their child everyday in a formal way, i.e. doing auditory training lessons, is such a trying experience for some mothers at the beginning that many mothers ask, "Do I really have to do lessons?"

Rather than answer this question directly, we will simply say that, generally, deaf children who develop good language and speech are those whose mothers have worked with them systematically to develop their language from the time their hearing losses were diagnosed.

Every mother and child is different; therefore there is no magic formula for making lessons successful. Every mother must establish a routine that suits her and her child.

Some mothers sit down for a lesson with their child only once a day, covering several words and ideas at one time. Others sit down several times a day for a very brief lesson (perhaps as short as five or ten minutes) which covers only one or two ideas. Most mothers make some plan in advance so that when they do sit down for the lessons they know what they are going to do. Some of us do a lesson every day of the week including Saturdays and Sundays. Others do formal lessons only on weekdays and take weekends off. Some do our lesson early in the morning to take advantage of our child's alterness; others do it after supper or just before bed. Frankly, it has taken some of us in this book as long as two years to become organized and settled into a comfortable and satisfying lesson routine.

1. What goes on in a lesson

Most mothers do something similar to the formal lessons described by a teacher of the deaf on pages 75-86.

a) We sit beside, not across from, our child;

b) We hold the hearing aid which is attached to a long cord (usually 36 inches) so that we can speak four to eight inches from the microphone and so that we don't have to speak loudly or exaggerate our voices;

c) We do a number of simple activities or games which will enable us to repeat over and over and over again the words or ideas we are concentrating on at that time.

2. What are you trying to teach your child in each lesson?

Generally, you are teaching your child language. BUT, you want him to learn language through the auditory channel, i.e. through listening, the way people with normal hearing learn it. Thus, your first weeks or even months of auditory training will be devoted to taking your child through the initial stages of language learning:

a) He has first to realize that sound exists and that not all sounds are the same.

b) He has to discover that sounds have meanings and in order to do this he has to discriminate one sound from another. In other words, he not only has to learn to hear the sound "bu bu bu" but he has to learn that the sound "bu bu bu" means "bus" and not "airplane" or "cow" or "rabbit". And that the sound "ah———" means the airplane and not the bus or anything else. Many lesson activities which we will describe later will help him accomplish this important step on the road to language learning.

c) He becomes aware that some sounds convey much more meaning than others. He learns that certain sounds require him to respond in a certain way, e.g. the sound "hot" can mean "don't touch"; the sound "stop" can mean that he is to stop what he is doing.

d) He learns that by making certain sounds himself he can

manipulate his environment and make things happen. For example, if he says "up", something will go up or he will be picked up. It takes many, many months for some children to make their first attempts at speech but certain games described later will encourage them to do so.

Once a child has learned that sound has meaning, then his training becomes largely a matter of vocabulary building and refining his listening skills. He learns more and more words and phrases and sounds and he learns to hear them from farther away. And in an auditory training program such as we have been involved in, all the vocabulary building is done through the use of natural language. The mother always speaks in sentences and phrases so that the child is exposed to a great variety of language patterns with their different rhythms, pauses, pitch, stress and intonation and the words are presented in many different ways and many contexts. For example, consider the many ways the word "low" can be used. "Stand on the lowest step", "Put it on the low shelf", "Move the picture lower down", "The clouds are low", "Listen to the low sound", "The baby has three lower teeth", "This is a low table", "Turn the light lower". Many words in English are like this. They have a basic meaning but many extended meanings.

3. Where to begin

The first sounds the teacher at the Hospital gave all of us to work on in lessons were "bu bu bu" for the bus, "ah———" for the airplane, and a few animal sounds. Simple concepts such as "up" and "down", "bye-bye", "all gone", "round and round", were also introduced in the first few lessons. I think that these sounds and words were chosen first because they are easy to hear and say and also because most children like them. They are words and phrases which have been observed in the early speech of normal children. As the child begins to listen, the words chosen are those thought to be the most useful to the child in handling his environment. The words and concepts are not necessarily given to each child in the same order and each child progresses at a

53

different rate. Probably a good rule of thumb in choosing words is that when you notice that your child needs or could use a word, teach it to him; however, DO NOT TRY TO TEACH HIM EVERYTHING HE NEEDS TO KNOW ALL AT ONCE IN LESSONS. Proceed slowly in your lessons. You can and should talk about many things with him casually around the house all day but in your lessons just do a few things at a time. In our first three months of auditory training, the only sounds and words my child and I worked on in lessons were:

bu bu bu (bus)	*baby*
ah——— (airplane)	*cup*
hop, hop, hop (rabbit)	*boat*
quack, quack (duck)	*car*
meow (cat)	*apple*
moo (cow)	*bird*
bow wow (dog)	*chair*
baa (sheep)	*eyes*
peep, peep, peep (chick)	*nose*
flower	*mouth*
shoe	*round and round*
ball	*loud and soft*
all gone	*bye bye*

One mother and child spent seven months on these first few words while another mother and child spent only two months.

During the next six months (in my case only), only about 40 new words were added in lessons at the rate of one or two, occasionally three a week; some action words, *(run, jump, fall down, blow, wash, open, close, push, pull)*; a few adjectives, *(hot* and *cold, wet* and *dry, fast* and *slow)* and names of more things with which the child came into contact almost every day, *(table, banana, orange, juice, water, cookie, pail, shovel, umbrella, soap, towel, house, bathtub, door, window, fish, box, hammer)*.

Lesson activities

1. A surprise box

Take a box big enough to put your hand in. Leave one end
open and cut a hole in the top, big enough for a hand-sized
toy to pop through. Let's assume you are working on "bu
bu bu", "hop, hop, hop" and "peep, peep, peep". Put a toy
bus, rabbit and chick in the box so that the child cannot see
them. Put your hand in the open end of the box and then
move it in front of the child but just out of his reach. Say
"bu bu bu, the bus goes bu bu bu", a couple of times and
then be quiet for a second or two. Then dramatically pop
the bus through the hole, making the "bu bu bu" sound
again. Let the child play with the bus for a few seconds so
you can repeat the sound again, then take the bus and put it
to the side. If he is reluctant to give up the bus, direct his
attention to the box to give him the idea that something
else might pop out.

Repeat this for the chick and the rabbit and then line up the
three toys in front of the child and ask for them as follows:
"Give me the bus that says bu bu bu ... bu bu bu ..." At
first, he probably won't know what you want him to do so
you will have to pick up the bus and drop it back into the
box yourself. Then ask for the second and third toys.
Eventually, he will get the idea that he is supposed to put
the toys back in the box as they are called for.

2. Variations on the surprise box

a) Cut a slit in the front of the box and place a picture of
each of the objects which are inside the box in front of
the child. Then show the child that as you say the
sound, you want him to put the appropriate picture
through the slit. If he puts the correct picture through,
the actual toy will pop up through the hole in the top to
surprise him. If he puts the incorrect picture through,
nothing happens. He will soon catch on. Some children
simply enjoy mailing the pictures as you make the
sound. You don't always have to use the objects.

b) When the child is a little older, you can let him reach into the box and try to find the toy you have asked for by using touch only—don't let him peek. Use the box in this way again much later when your child is learning textures. You will then be asking him to, "find something that is rough", "find something that is soft", etc. Eventually, but this comes much later, you can put two or more of the same objects in the box and ask him to reach in and find two or three things that are "alike".

c) Wrap two or three objects separately in paper (newspaper will do—young children are not fussy) and place them in a box. For example, if you are teaching your child "car", wrap up three little cars; then remove the first package from the box and in a very surprised and excited tone of voice say something like "Look what I have found. Maybe it's a car. I wonder if it's a car. Let's unwrap it and see if it is a car. I hope it's a car". As you unwrap the car, keep talking like this, **IN PHRASES AND SENTENCES BUT REPEATING THE WORD "CAR" AS OFTEN AS YOU CAN.** Then, the big moment. "It is a car! What do you know! A car. Here's the car. You can play with the car. You like cars. Cars are fun". etc. Let him fiddle with the car a little so you can keep talking about it. Then persuade him to park the car by showing him that there is something else wrapped up in the box. Then you begin all over again. "Oh look, I wonder what this is. Maybe it's another car", etc. Let him unwrap this one so that you can repeat all the language you used the first time into the microphone and then on to the third. By the time you have finished this game your child will have heard the word "car" at least a hundred times. **And this is the kind of repetition which a hearing impaired child needs.**

A variation of this unwrapping game is to use three or four objects instead of just one. One parcel may contain a car, another a boat, the third a flower, for example.

3. Take three or four yoghurt containers with lids (any kind of small container will do) and, before the lesson, place one of

the objects you are working with into each container. For example, one might contain a doll's shoe, another a boat, another an airplane and the last one a cat. For the lesson, line these up beside you, out of the child's reach; then take each one in turn, shake it and listen so the child may hear the object banging against the sides of the container. Let the child shake it so that he can hear and feel there is something in it. All the while you are talking to him just as in the game in which you unwrap the cars. "What's in it? Maybe it's a shoe. Let's open it up. See if it's a shoe", etc. Help the child open the container if he cannot do it himself and then let him fiddle with the shoe for a litte while so you can keep talking about it. Then place the shoe to the side and begin all over again with the container that has the airplane inside and so on.

A variation of this is simply to place the containers upside-down to cover the objects and to ask the child to find the object you are asking for. "Where's the shoe? Can you find the shoe?". When he finds the shoe, pat him on the head and possibly even reward him with a small treat and then ask him to find another object.

You can purchase colored plastic eggs in a toy shop which are also excellent for this type of surprise game. When a child takes each egg apart, he discovers an object inside.

4. Make a small chest of drawers by taping three or four cigarette boxes, or 'Q'-tip boxes, together. Use small split paper fasteners to make the handles on the drawers. Then in each drawer place a picture of one of the objects you are working with. Open each drawer in turn and let the child remove the picture and look at it while you talk about it into the hearing aid microphone. "Here's a cow. Moo——— the cow says moo———" and so on. After he has looked at the picture for a while, ask him to do something specific with it such as put in on a flannel board which you have propped up beside him; or mail it in a mail box; or hang it on a hook. You can make a flannel board simpy by attaching a piece of flannelette fabric to a piece of heavy cardboard and attaching a cardboard flap at the back to hold it

upright (see diagram). You can make a hook board by screwing four to six cup hooks into a piece of wood about 12" x 12" square.

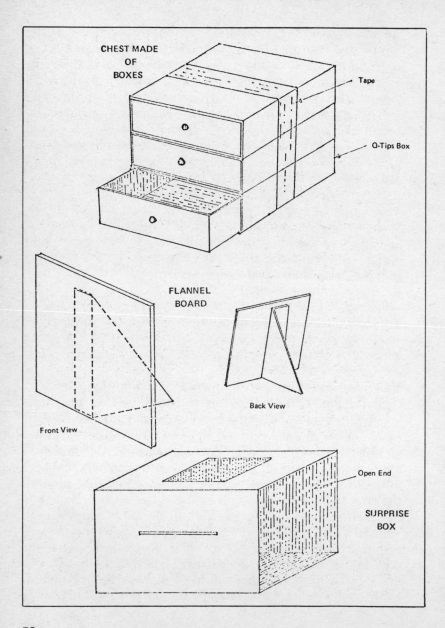

CHEST MADE
OF
BOXES

Tape

Q-Tips Box

FLANNEL
BOARD

Back View

Front View

Open End

SURPRISE
BOX

All of these props—the chest, the flannel board and the hook board can be used in a number of different ways to develop your child's auditory discrimination. Here are a few examples of what you can do:—

a) Turn the chest upside down and pull the drawers out to different lengths to make a small staircase. Then take a miniature doll or animal and stand it at the bottom of the steps. Pause for a moment and then say, "up", and move the doll up. You want the child to realize that the doll moves only after the sound "up". After you move the doll up the stairs a few times this way, hold the hearing aid microphone in front of the child's mouth, trying to encourage him to make the sound "up" so that the action will occur. Eventually he learns that in order to get action he has to make a sound.

b) Stick miniature marshmallows on the cup hook board. When he hears the signal—it may simply be the word "go"—he is allowed to remove a marshmallow from one of the hooks and eat it.

c) Place the flannel board directly in front of the child. Have at the side a number of pictures of something you are trying to teach your child, for example, "baby". Pass him the first picture and say, "Here's a baby . . . A baby . . . Such a lovely baby . . . Put the baby up here", and direct him to put the picture of the baby up on the flannel board and then go on to the next picture. "Here's another baby . . . See the baby . . . That's right . . . Put the baby up there", and so on. By the time he has finished putting up five or six pictures of babies up on the board, you will have had a chance to use the word "baby" fifty or sixty times close to the microphone of his hearing aid.

d) Place four or five pictures in front of the child and, as you call for the pictures, one at a time, he can mount them on the flannel board. For example, place before him the pictures of a bus, a shoe, a flower, an airplane and a rabbit. "Where's the shoe? . . . Put the shoe here

... Good boy, that's the shoe", and so on. Always ask for the pictures in a different way.

5. An excellent way to teach that a sound produces action is to hang a toy animal over a doorway by a string which can be pulled to move the toy up or down from the other side of the door. One parent can stand holding the child while the other hides behind the door. The parent holding the child says "Up" clearly into the child's microphone and the other parent makes the animal move up. There is a pause and again the parent beside the child says "Up". The child will probably find this very amusing and eventually can be persuaded or may try to say "Up" himself to get the action.

Another game of this type is to have one parent lie down on the bed and pretend to be asleep. The mother and child stand beside the bed and then the mother says clearly into the hearing aid microphone, "Wake up". Daddy sits up in bed dramatically and then in a few seconds he lies down again. Once again, mother says, "Wake up", and Daddy sits up again. Then the parents can exchange places. Children generally love such games and you should play them over and over again whether the child says anything or not.

6. **Listening to the doorbell**

Have your child ring the doorbell. As soon as he rings it, open the door, saying something like, "I heard the doorbell!" Do it a few times then reverse the roles; the child is inside and you are outside; the door is shut. Instruct your child to listen for the doorbell; as soon as he hears it, he should open the door. Wait a few seconds before ringing to make certain that your child does not open the door without listening."

This game was greatly enjoyed by my son. Usually I was the one to say, "That's enough for now". Since he was too little to reach the doorbell, I usually put a chair or a stool outside to enable him to reach it.

A similar game can be played by knocking.

7. Listening to the telephone ring

Arrange with someone to call at a designated time of the day when you can have your child sitting quietly (or playing quietly), not more than three feet away from the telephone. At the very beginning explain to him that the telephone is going to ring soon and that he is to listen for it, (cup your hand to your ear or point to your ear, if you are not certain that he understands that you want him to listen). When the telephone starts to ring, ignore it, so as not to tip him off. If he appears not to notice, remind him that he is to listen; if he still gives no indication of having heard it, say something like, "I hear the telephone, I have to answer it".

I found it useless to repeat this exercise more than twice on the same day. In anticipation of the ring, my son would "hear" the telephone even if it was not ringing.

When he starts indicating that he hears the telephone on his own, have him playing quietly at the same distance as before, only now do not tell him you are expecting it to ring. Watch him closely for a reaction. If you are convinced he can hear it, you are ready to increase the distance from the telephone. Start by moving him five or six feet away. Later the game can be modified by listening from an adjoining room and maybe even further away. It is important to have the house free of other household sounds during this game.

8. The 'Go' game

This game can be played with a very young child as soon as he is able to listen and respond to simple commands. It helps him develop his listening skills and prepares him for the conventional hearing tests given by the audiologists.

The game is played as follows:

> *Mother sits beside the child holding the hearing aid six to eight inches from her mouth. The child is given a container filled with blocks and another*

empty container is placed in front of him. The child is instructed to take a block, hold it to his ear and wait until he hears the word "go". Upon hearing the word he is to put the block into the empty container. The game continues until all the blocks have been transferred in this manner or until the child loses interest.

The 'Go' game can be played with a variety of objects such as pegs to be put on the peg board; marbles to be dropped into an empty plastic milk jug; cars to be rolled down the ramp; apples to be placed from one basket to another; beads to be laced on a shoe lace; miniature marshmallows to be eaten off the hook board. For an action-minded child pieces of paper crumpled up and rolled into a ball can be thrown into a wastebasket standing some distance away from the child.

The game can be modified by substituting other commands or by using various sound signals; Mother can beat the drum, ring a bell, sound a buzzer, shake a rattle, blow a horn, etc.

9. Action games during lessons

Some children simply cannot sit still for very long, no matter how exciting you try to make your lessons. So you may wish to have one or two action games in every lesson. For example, with a young child, you can hide one of the objects you are working with and then go around the house together looking for it, all the while talking about it, e.g. "Where's the ball? Let's find the ball. Is the ball under here? No ball here ... Here's the ball! We found the ball. Let's take the ball back to the table". If you were working on the phrase "pick up", you could hide several objects around the house and then together go around picking them up and putting them in a container, all the while saying, "Let's pick up the car ... Pick up the car ... You picked up the car ... Now pick up the airplane ... Pick up the shoe, etc." Then take all the objects you picked up back to the table and perhaps use them in another activity.

Children seem to enjoy imitating any kind of action. For example, for a change of pace in a lesson, you can sit beside each other on the floor and repeat one or two actions over and over again following your instructions, e.g. "Lie down", "Sit up", "Lie down", "Sit up", over and over again. Most children find something like this great fun. Even something as simple as walking up and down the steps a few times is great fun for them. "Let's walk up; let's walk down". When you are teaching your child "hot" and "cold", you could walk to all the sinks and bathtubs in the house, turning on the hot and cold taps. At each one talk about "hot" and "cold". Then when you return to the table, you can place one container of hot and one of cold in front of him and ask him to identify the one you ask for.

After your child has learned a few simple instructions and is a little older, he can go away from the table and do as you instruct. For example, "Sit down", "Stand up", "Turn around", "Walk forward", "Walk backwards". Then, if he has started talking, he can give you the instructions.

10. Planned surprises

These are little events which a mother can plan but which seem to the child to occur as part of daily routines. For example, at night, hide a car or any other object which you may be working on in lessons in your child's sock. The next morning, when you are dressing him: "Oh my! There's something in your sock . . . What is it? . . . Maybe it's a car . . . Feel it . . . Is it a car? . . . etc." You continue to talk about the object as you remove it from his sock and then as he fiddles with it.

You can discover something in your sleeve, in your shoe, under his blanket when you are putting him to bed at night, in his cup when you are about to pour him some juice. If he is at the stage where he likes to open and empty all your kitchen drawers and cupboards every day, hide lesson objects in these places so that he can discover them and you can talk about them again. You can leave little boxes wrapped up like presents around the house for him to find.

When he brings them to you to open them up, you can again talk about the object which is inside. When he is having his nap, attach small objects or pictures around his crib so that he will discover them when he awakens and again you can talk about them.

You can no doubt think of many more surprises which you can plan for your child.

As you can see from these games, **the objective is to expose the child over and over again to sounds, words and phrases and to give him the opportunities to learn to discriminate these sounds from others by hearing only.**

Rather than continue to describe specific lesson games, we thought it would be most useful to discuss some other materials you can use when planning your lessons and how these might be used for teaching specific words and concepts. Also a discussion of materials to buy for lessons is included.

Household objects to use in lessons

1. **Use Kleenex:** Crumple it up and then blow it across the table to teach "blow". Later, use it to teach "crumple", "fold", "tear" and "torn", "rip", "wrap", etc.

2. **Use oranges, grapefruit, bananas, apples** in your lessons to teach, "cut", "squeeze", "slice", "peel". When children are around two-and-a-half they love to try to cut with scissors or knives and you can allow them to do this in lessons because you are supervising them; they will be unlikely to hurt themselves. For example, to teach, "cut", you cut an organge into sections first and then let the child cut the sections into smaller pieces. (He may become frustrated trying to cut up the whole orange). As this is going on, you can talk into the microphone of the hearing aid about "cutting" over and

over again. The next day cut up a banana, and then the third day an apple or a piece of celery. Your child will not lose interest if he finds the activity challenging.

3. **Gather up several household objects to teach one idea.** For example to teach "sharp", collect into one container a pair of pointed scissors, a sharpened pencil, a paring knife, a straight pin, a needle, a safety pin, etc. Show the child each object in turn and let him feel that each is sharp. All the while, of course, you are talking about this quality of the objects. For example, "Here's something that is sharp . . . This pencil is sharp . . . Feel it . . . See how sharp it is . . . It is sharp . . . Very sharp". By the time you have gone through all the objects in the container in this way, your child will have heard the word "sharp" fifty to a hundred times.

In this way you can teach other concept language: *colors, shapes, what things are made of, old, new, torn, faded, big* and *little, dirty* and *clean.*

Some mothers when they began teaching certain concept words such as colors and shapes, *used objects which were identical in all respects expect for the concept being taught.* For example, for "dirty" and "clean" they used two identical boots, one of which was dirty and one clean; two identical cups, one of which was dirty and one clean; two identical spoons, one clean and one dirty, etc. They feel that it is important to do this initially so that the child will not be confused. Similarly, when they first began to teach colors, they used objects which were identical in all respects, except their color.

4. **Use water** in lessons to teach many, many things such as *full* and *empty, spill, wipe it up, wet* and *dry, hot* and *cold, splash, sink* and *float, deep* and *shallow.* To take *full* and *empty* as an example, have a jug of water within your reach and place two empty cups in front of the child. Then fill one up and say, "This cup is full; now it's full." Then show the other cup is still empty and pour the water out of the cup into the jug and say,

"Now the cup is empty." Repeat this with two glasses and with other containers. After you have done this once or twice, let the child fill one up so that you can reinforce the language again. Little children between the ages of two and three usually love pouring water and enjoy this simple activity.

A variation is to use juice when teaching such things as "pouring", "full" and "empty", "drink", etc. When you have finished demonstrating the idea you are working on, let the child drink the juice for a pleasant break in the lesson. If you use small plastic cups (the toy kind) you and your child can play a tea party type of game, taking turns pouring juice for each other to drink. This will enable you to use the words "pour" and "drink" about forty or fifty times in five minutes as you talk about what you are doing.

To teach "spill" simply have a cloth handy and knock over onto the table a small plastic glass with water in it and then wipe it up, all the while describing what is happening. "Oh dear, it spilled; the water spilled. Wipe it up. I'm wiping it up". The child will just love taking his turn at spilling the water and wiping it up, and again as he does so, you can describe into the microphone of the hearing aid what is going on.

Wash a doll in a small basin of water to teach the parts of the body. You do it first, talking as you go along. "Let's wash her face. I'm washing her face; now wash her hands, wash her hands" etc. When you have finished, the child can wash the doll and you can again repeat all the language into the hearing aid microphone as he does so.

Use a small basin of soapy water for teaching "wash" and also the names of clothing: "Wash your sock . . . Now wash the other sock . . . Wash your shorts . . . Wash your mitts . . . etc." You can wash the item first as the child watches and then as he has his turn, you can repeat into his microphone all the language you used when you did it the first time. Teach "blowing bubbles" with the same water.

Make a slide going into a basin of water by propping up a piece of wood or piece of heavy cardboard for the slide. Place a few objects that you are concentrating on in front of the child one at a time telling about them as you do so. "Here's a duck ... Quack, quack ... The duck says quack, quack, quack", and so on. When all the objects are in front of the child you ask him for them one at a time. "Where's the duck that goes quack, quack, quack?" When he picks up the duck direct him to let it go down the slide into the water. Children love this game.

5. **Use foods such as jam, honey, corn syrup, lemons, sugar and salt,** to teach such concept words as "tastes", i.e. "tastes sweet", "tastes sour", "sticky", "gooey", "rotten", "mouldy". For example, place two blank pieces of paper in front of the child or place two small cups in front of the child, one filled with sweetened orange juice and the other filled with unsweetened lemon juice. First taste the sweet one and talk about how sweet it tastes. (Do the sweet one first because he may not want to try another one if he first tastes the sour lemon). Then taste the other one. You can take turns tasting and talking until the juice is all gone, or you can end the game by asking the child which one he wants to drink. No doubt he will choose the sweet one. For other tasts use sugar and salt, cocoa and sugar, sweetened and unsweetened chocolate.

6. **Collect natural objects** for use in lessons such as stones, acorns, chestnuts, sea shells, twigs and many other useful things which can be picked up outside. For example, when you are just beginning you can fill an old coffee can with stones to make a noisy toy, shake it and say, "Listen, can you hear that?" Then shake it again; let the child shake it. You can show him what is in the can and indicate that the noise occurs when the stones bang against the side of the can. Dried out twigs are useful for

teaching "break it".

When the child is learning to count, such objects are useful. For example, when the child is first learning to understand numbers, place three pieces of paper, each of which has a circle drawn on it in front of the child. In the circle on the first paper, write the number one; in the circle on the second paper, write the number two and in the third circle write the number three. Then help the child put the appropriate number of stones or shells or acorns or whatever into each circle. Once he gets the idea, let him repeat the activity by himself and then ask him to give you the number of stones you ask for. Insects and plants are invaluable for teaching "dead", "alive" and "dying". Dried dandelions are great for "blow".

Materials to buy for lessons

1. Miniature people, animals, furniture, vehicles

The reason miniature objects are suggested is that they are easy to manipulate, both by mother and child. Also they can be hidden in things, and under things and placed on top of things, or lined up in rows all within the child's reach on a table.

A miniature family is especially good; a man, woman, boy and girl, particularly if the dolls are flexible. After the child learns, "man", "woman", "girl" and "boy", these can be used to teach prepositions. He can learn to "Put the man on the chair", "Put the girl on the table", "Put the boy on the car", etc, when he hears these instructions.

Again, these might be used when the child is learning such verbs as "lead" and "follow". He can line up the dolls according to specific instructions such as, "Make the girl follow the boy . . . Make the man follow the girl . . . etc."

No doubt you can think of many, many other words and

concepts which can be demonstrated by using these miniature objects.

2. Plasticine

You and your child can model things together, making cars, buses, small animals and other objects and talking about each object as you make it. "I'm making an airplane . . . ah——— . . . See my airplane . . . ah——— . . ."

Later, many concepts such as "thick" and "thin" can be demonstrated with plasticine. The child can be given a small rolling pin, some cookie cutters, or a knife to cut the plasticine with. This enables you to teach him such instructions as, "roll it out", "press it down", "lift it up", "turn it over". Or you can shape the basic object, e.g. a cat or a cup or an airplane or an elephant and ask the child to make some, "whiskers for the cat", "a handle for the cup", "wings for the airplane", "a trunk for the elephant".

It is really not necessary to buy plasticine. Play dough can be used in the same way. Make it by mixing three cups of flour, one cup of salt, one cup of water and a quarter of a cup of vegetable oil—children love to help make it. This in itself can be a language lesson because you have to, "Pour in the water", "Pour in the oil", "Knead it" to "Make it smoother".

3. Wooden blocks

A good set of colored wooden blocks can be used in lessons for years. There are many ways of using them from the time your child begins auditory training and is learning simple concepts such as "up" and "down" until he is quite a bit older and learning such things as "every other one", "all except", etc.

For example, at the beginning, build a stairway using the blocks and make a small doll or animal walk "up" and "down", "up" and "down". Or have the child take a number of blocks out of a pail and pile them on shelves, the first one "up" on the top shelf, the next one "down" on the bottom shelf.

Two blocks can be banged together to make a "loud" sound and then gently to make a "soft" sound.

Blocks can be stacked to make a "high" tower and then you can "knock it over". (Needless to say, this is a great favorite with most children!).

Blocks can be used for teaching colors, for counting and for prepositions. For example, you can build a bridge out of blocks and make cars and animals go "under the bridge". You can make a car or an animal go "around and around and around" a block. When you are teaching "drop", you can play a game dropping the blocks one by one from the table on to the floor. Then you have to "pick up" the blocks. Children usually find this very amusing.

4. **Construction and drawing paper, crayons, colored pencils, sticky paper, etc.**

For many mothers, drawing is a major medium for auditory training. You can either draw and just describe what you are drawing to your child as you go along; or you can create certain drawing activites in which the child can draw too. For example, if you were teaching "mouth", trace several (six to ten) circles on a plain piece of paper and on each circle draw two eyes and a nose but no mouth. When you produce this paper during the lesson, talk to the child about the fact that there is no mouth on each face. Draw in the mouth on one of the faces and then let the child draw the mouths on the other faces. As he does so, you can keep using the word "mouth" in many different ways. "Put a mouth on this face . . . This face has no mouth . . . There's the mouth . . . Now this face needs a mouth", etc. You can use the word "mouth" about 20 times in an exercise like this and many children can draw something that resembles a mouth in roughly the right place on a face when they are two to two-and-a-half years old.

This same type of drawing activity can be used for teaching the names of the parts of things. For example, to teach "handle", draw several cups without handles and let the child draw the handles. Draw buses without "wheels" and let the child draw the "wheels". Draw houses without doors and let the child put on the doors. Draw faces, again without mouths, and let the child make them "happy" or "sad" when you are teaching these concepts.

Another type of lesson game which allows you to repeat one word or concept many, many times is building up pictures out of construction paper either with paste or sticky paper. For example, assume you are working on the word "star". Take a black or dark blue piece of construction paper. Before the lesson begins, cut out a yellow crescent moon, a house, a tree and a number of stars (10 to 20). Then during the lesson take out the paper and say to your child, "It's night time. The moon is shining", and paste the moon on to the dark paper. Stick the house in the bottom corner of the picture and put the tree beside it, describing what you are doing. Then say, "The stars are shining. Here's a star", and paste on a star. You can then say, "There are lots of stars . . . Look at all the stars . . . Do you want to put the stars on? . . . Here, you put a star on . . .", and at this point the child takes over pasting each star in the sky as you hand it to him and talk about it. This sort of thing can be put up on the kitchen wall after the lesson and shown to Daddy when he comes home so that the word "star" can be reviewed again.

This same sort of picture building activity can be used for teaching the parts of a house, "door", "window", "chimney", etc. and for such things as "petals" on flowers, "rays" on the sun, "whiskers" on a cat or rabbit etc.

5. Books

Books are so important for language development through auditory training that we have devoted an entire section of this book to them (see Part II — Auditory Training Through Books, page 101.

6. A camera

A camera is a must! Among the many things you can teach your child with pictures you have taken are:—

a) Names:
Take straightforward passport type photographs of all the members of the family, including grandparents, aunts, uncles, cousins, etc. In fact, take pictures of all the people with whom your child regularly comes into contact so that you can review their names over and over again to help your child learn them. This is especially important when your child begins nursery school and you want him to learn the names of his teachers and classmates.

b) Relationships:
You can teach your child family relationships using the same pictures you used for teaching him names: for example, grandmother, grandfather, aunt, uncle, teacher, etc.

c) Place names:
Take photographs of all the places you regularly visit, i.e. supermarket, drug store, service station, etc., to help him learn these words and the phrases people say there such as, "Fill it up" . . . "Do you have any blueberry ice cream?"

d) Time concepts:
(1) The Seasons: Photograph your child in the same place—perhaps in front of your house—during each season to teach and later review the names of the seasons. This is also a chance to review language of temperatures, special clothing and activities suitable to each season.

(2) Vacations and trips: Look at your summer vacation pictures a few times over the winter to reinforce such phrases as, "Last summer we went to . . .", "Do you remember when . . . ?" "Last July . . .", or "Last year . . ." Or look at your Christmas pictures in spring and

summer.

(3) Special occasions: The names of Christmas, Easter, Halloween, etc. can be reviewed through photographs. Details can be taken to discuss whether or not we shall do the same thing again this year or not.

(4) Time and change: Here old photographs help. All children love to talk of "When I was a baby," "When Mommy was in Grade 3", or "When Mommy and Daddy got married" etc. The family album is, in fact, an invaluable source of language building material.

7. Puzzles, toys and games

It is not necessary to buy everything you see labelled "Educational Toy", but a few games and toys are useful for variety in lessons. A few games which are fun for very young children are:

a) *Hickety Pickety* by Parker Brothers
b) *Hi-ho! Cherry-O* by Whitman
c) *Candy Land* by Milton Bradley Company.

Some games and puzzles are especially good for vocabulary building:

a) *Lotto Games*
b) *Ed-U-Games* by Ed-U-Cards
c) *Go-Together Match-ups* by Playschool
d) *Sequence Cards* by Milton Bradley

8. Newspapers, magazines, weekend comics and old school readers

Leaf through your daily paper and subscription magazines as a constant source of new and interesting pictures to illustrate lesson words.

The weekend comics, especially *Nancy, Henry, Hi & Lois* and *Family Circus* are excellent for story sequencing activities. You can cut up frames and, after discussion, ask the child to arrange them in the correct order of first, second, third, etc.

An excellent source of pictures for lesson words is old grade school readers and the workbooks which accompany these. They can be obtained from teachers at your local school. Often people donate them for school Fun Fairs and Bazaars, where they can be purchased for a nominal cost (five or ten cents each). They are so inexpensive that you do not mind cutting them up.

When your child reaches three-and-a-half to four years of age a good source of interesting lesson material is *Highlights*, the monthly magazine for children. Order this through Highlights for Children Inc., P.O. Box 269, Columbus, Ohio, 43216.

9. **The Canadian Association of Toy Libraries** is located at 50 Quebec Avenue, Suite 1207, Toronto, Ontario M6P 4B4.

We could go on and on describing lesson games and materials but what we have described will give you an idea of where and how to begin, and, most important of all, we hope that your own imagination has been set to work.

As one mother said in her story, "You'll be surprised at what you can come up with."

Just remember, go slowly in your lessons at first; do not try to do all the things suggested here all at once; and do not be disappointed if many of the ideas do not work for you—every mother has to find her own style.

Auditory training
- A teacher's
approach

by Louise Crawford

When preparing lessons for hearing impaired children, there are certain principles that I generally follow.

Before discussing these principles and outlining two sample lessons, I would like to describe the conditions under which I work.

I teach in a clinical setting and see only one child at a time. Because I am training the mother to teach her hearing impaired child at home, she stays for the lesson and the three of us work together. We sit at a large table and the child is on my right. Little children are seated in a high chair; older ones sit on an ordinary chair. The mother sits opposite us. **The reason I sit beside the child, not opposite him, is to minimize the opportunities for him to watch my face for lipreading clues. I want to give him the chance to develop speech and language primarily through the auditory channel (i.e. listening), not the visual channel (lipreading).**

I keep my toys and teaching materials in containers on the floor and in drawers on my left where they are out of the child's sight but within my reach. I use the child's own hearing aid for amplification. Most of the children are fitted with body-type hearing aids. I hold the aid in my hand because I prefer to talk about four inches from the microphone so that the child has the best possible opportunity to hear what is being said. I replace the child's short cord with a 36-inch cord to give us both more freedom of movement. If the child is fitted binaurally, I usually hold one aid and use a long Y cord so that he will continue to have amplification in both ears.

To ensure that a lesson goes smoothly, I think it is essential to plan it in advance and to have all the necessary props such as pictures, toys, books and puzzles within my reach before I begin. I keep a separate folder for each child which contains his lesson plans and lists of vocabulary which we have covered in the past and are currently doing. The folder is placed on the table beside me where I can refer to it and jot down my comments or ideas that occur to me and might be helpful in planning future lessons. I do not always follow the lesson I have planned. Sometimes the mood of the child or an interesting point that crops up leads us off in another direction. However, the lesson is always there to fall back on so that I do not find myself in the position of floundering around wondering what to do next while the child is becoming restless and losing interest.

Very young children and older ones in the early stages of language development often have short attention spans. To maintain the child's interest and co-operation I usually move fairly rapidly from one activity to another stopping each one before the child has an opportunity to become bored by it. I think it is important to vary the types of props used during a given lesson: i.e. I try not to plan too many activities involving the use of pictures but, rather, include toys, books, and real objects that can be handled and manipulated to illustrate my points. I try to arrange the activities so that I move from one that requires the child to listen attentively and respond to one in which he is allowed to play with the material in his own fashion or merely to listen passively. Finally, when asking the child to pick out objects or pictures to test his language comprehension, it is best to include some very familiar items with the newer ones. I usually ask for one of the familiar items first to get off to a good start and keep the others in reserve. Then if he makes a few incorrect responses and begins to become discouraged, I can give him a chance for an easy success by asking for something he knows very well in an attempt to restore his confidence.

Now I will describe two sample lessons. The first is designed for a hearing impaired child who has neither language comprehension nor speech. He could be as young as 12 months of age. I start the children with the sounds of the bus and the airplane saying that the bus goes "bu bu bu " and the airplane goes "ah———" (as in "paw"). I have explained to the parent that I have found these sounds easy to hear and to imitate, and we want to give their child every chance to be successful so we will begin with something easy. I also use a few animal sounds because they have strong rhythmic patterns which are easy to distinguish. I counsel the parents to say the animal sounds with expression as though they really were the animal itself. I include *up* and *down, round and round, stop* and *all gone* because there are many obvious ways to illustrate these basic concepts. Most children enjoy playing with balls and have one at home so the word "ball" is included in the initial lesson.

Sample lesson A

1. Play with the airplane and the bus

These toys are produced one at a time. I say the appropriate sound *before* I show each one to the child (bu bu bu for the bus and ah ——— for the airplane). As he is looking at each one and as he plays with it for a few moments I continue to say the sounds into the aid. Then I produce a

The airplane says "ah———".

plastic toy pail and indicate that I want the toys placed in the pail as I call for them. Usually, he does not initially understand what is required when I first say "bu bu bu", so I place the objects in the pail myself making the appropriate sound as I pick up each object. (I have found that if I always use the same pail for collecting the objects the child quickly learns what is expected when he sees it and is saved considerable confusion).

"Bu bu bu ... the bus says "bu bu bu".

2. Play with the merry-go-round

I say, "Here is something that goes round and round" and then show the child a toy merry-go-round (a quiet top would do as well). I place the toy on the table out of the child's reach where he can see it but not grab it. As it spins I talk about the fact that it is going round and round and move my finger with a circular motion on the top of the table. As it comes to a stand still I put up my hand as would a policeman and say "Stop". I repeat this activity a few times but put the toy away before the child has lost interest in it. (I think it is important to talk about the toy before showing it to the child. Once he has been presented with it, he may become so absorbed in looking at the toy or manipulating it that he fails to listen to the language that describes it.)

I use this activity time and again until the day comes when I say "Here is something that goes round and round", and the child either looks to the place on the shelf where I keep the merry-go-round or else he moves his finger in the circular motion to indicate that he has understood.

3. Play with a toy cow, airplane and cat which have been hidden in plastic eggs

The child is handed one egg at a time. If he does not want to open the egg I do it for him. As each toy is exposed, I talk about it and make the appropriate sound. I then put the eggs aside and place the three objects in front of the child. If he tries to grab and throw them, I place them slightly out of his reach. Then I produce the toy pail and naming each object encourage the child to help me put it in the pail. When this task is accomplished, I place the pail on the table and present the child with the eggs. He is encouraged to put them back together one at a time. When he has done so with whatever help is required from me, I bring the pail forward again and putting my hand in, take out one toy at a time giving the appropriate sound before I bring it

"Here's a bus . . . bu bu bu".

into view and repeating that sound a few times before I put it away. When all the toys have been removed I turn the pail over dramatically and comment on the fact that the toys are "all gone".

"Ah——— the airplane says ah———".

"The cow says moo . . . moo".

4. Talk about a book

I have selected a book in which there are attractive pictures of animals. There is only one animal presented on each page. As I show the child each picture, I make the appropriate sound. If the child tries to grab the book I hold it slightly out of his reach. If his attention span is very short, I show him only those pages on which the particular animals we are studying are pictured.

5. Play with a toy cat

I have a toy cat that walks down an inclined plane. I say, "Here is a cat that says 'meow'." I show him the cat and as he watches it walk down the inclined board a few times, I repeat the sound "meow". Then I put the toy away.

6. Play with a xylophone

I have a xylophone which produces pleasing tones. We play with it for a while. It is a pleasant listening experience and provides both the child and teacher with a change from animals, buses and airplanes.

7. Play with a stick to teach "up" and "down"

I present a brightly colored stick. Holding it away from the child so that he cannot grab it, I raise it up saying "up" and lower it again saying "down". This activity is repeated several times, but stopped before the child loses interest.

8. Play with a cow puzzle

I say, "Here is the cow that says 'moo'," and produce the puzzle. If the child is not yet able to do the puzzle himself, I do it for him. Before putting it away, I have managed to say "moo" several times.

9. Play with a sheep and a noise maker

I have a noise maker that produces a "baa" sound when it is

turned over. I say, "I have a sheep that says 'baa'." I present my toy sheep and the noisemaker. After I have said "baa" a few times we listen to the noisemaker and if the child wants to, he is allowed to manipulate it.

10. Play with a simple form box

If the child has developed sufficiently to benefit from the activity, I present him with a simple form box. He is shown how to fit the various shapes in the holes. The children usually enjoy playing with this toy and it is an activity designed to bring the lesson to a happy close.

The second lesson which I will describe is designed for a child who has had one or two years of listening experience and auditory training. He, his mother, and I are old friends by this time and used to working together. His language comprehension is developing steadily and he now uses many single words spontaneously and perhaps some short phrases. His mother has been working on perhaps eight or ten specific words and concepts during the week. I have included these in my lesson.

Sample lesson B

1. Check on vocabulary that has been previously assigned for study at home.

I present eight different pictures and objects, each of which illustrates a specific word or concept. As I present each one we talk about it. Two of the items illustrate old familiar words for review. The others illustrate newer language that we hope the child has learned during the week at home. The child is encouraged to say the desired word if he is able; if not, he is only required to listen to it. When all of the items have been placed on the table in front of the child, I have the child turn his head away or else cover my face so that he cannot read my lips and, speaking close to the microphone of the hearing aid, ask for the various things. If he is unable to give the correct response, I repeat the direction and show him which item I have requested.

Example:

One of the words to be checked is "drip". The child's mother has already shown water dripping from a tap at home. I present a picture of some water dripping from a pair of hands. I say, "Look, what's this?" If there is no response, I say, "It is some water dripping. Can you say 'drip'?" If the child responds, I praise him. If not, I do not insist, but just repeat the language for him to hear. "Look, there is some water dripping."

Then, when asking the child to pick out the picture from the others in the group, I say, "Can you show me something that is dripping?" **Notice that I do not use the word "water" this time. I am testing his comprehension of the word "dripping". If I mention "water" he may select the correct picture on the basis of having heard and understood that familiar word and I still will not know whether or not he comprehends, "dripping". Nor do I consider one correct response proof that a child fully comprehends a word or concept. He must be able to give consistent correct responses with different materials in different contexts over a period of time.**

Notice also that I use both "drip" and "dripping" when speaking to the child so that he will learn that both words convey the same general meaning.

2. Work with the preposition "under".

This is a familiar activity to the child which has been repeated to review the proposition "under" but also to provide an opportunity to develop the child's auditory memory. Four familiar items such as a box, a table, a chair and a cup are placed in a row in front of the child. He is asked to turn the cup and the box upside down. Then I place six little toys such as a flower, a dog, a shoe, a car, a mouse and an elephant in a group in front of me.

As each object is brought into view the child is given the opportunity to name it but not pressured into doing so. Then the child is asked to listen to and follow the directions: "Put the mouse under the chair", "Put the shoe under the box" etc. If he is unable to follow the direction on the second or third try he is shown what to do. **Notice that this exercise requires him to listen for two things, the name of the object and the place where it is to be put.**

When the child has placed each item as directed, I put a plastic container on the table beside him and give his mother his hearing aid to hold. I stand about eight feet behind him and say, "Find the flower", "Find the key", etc. In response to each direction the child is required to place the correct object in the container. This exercise gives him practice in listening to familiar words at a distance from the speaker. If he is unable to respond correctly I move closer to him and repeat the direction. If he still is unable to respond, I take the hearing aid from his mother, repeat what I have said once more close to the microphone and if necessary point to the desired object.

3. **Introduce the concepts of "people" and "animals".**

The child already knows the names of many animals and the words "boy", "girl", "man", "woman" and "baby". I place two blank sheets of paper in front of him; I point to the one on the left and tell him that is for the "people". I point to the one on the right and tell him that this is for the animals. I have a container full of toy animals and people. I take a boy and say, "Here is a boy. The boy is one of the people", and place it on the paper on the left. Then I show him a dog and say, "I have a dog. A dog is an animal", and place it on the paper on the right. When we have finished sorting out all the objects in the container, I ask the child to show me the people and show me the animals and encourage him to say these words.

4. **Check on the child's comprehension of the direction, "Look behind you!"**

During the week the mother has been teaching her child the

direction, "Look behind you!" I suddenly say to him, "Look behind you!" If he does not respond, I say to his mother, "Mommy, look behind you." She complies and then I say to the child again, "Look behind you!" and hope that he will respond appropriately.

5. **Check on the child's comprehension of the directions "Turn it around" and "Knock it over".**

Previously the child had been taught the direction "Turn it around." Later, he was taught "Knock it over." Now I want to see if he is able to distinquish between those two directions. I take a rectangular block and stand it on its end and I say "Turn it around." If the child does not respond, I show him what to do. If he responds correctly, I praise him and say "Now, knock it over."

6. **Play a matching game**

The first, second, third and fourth activities of this lesson have required the child to listen carefully; he needs a rest. This matching game is a reading readiness activity and provides an opportunity to review familiar language and expose the child to new language. I show the child a big picture of a child's bedroom full of toys. I have some little pictures of some of the objects present in the bedroom scene. I show him a little picture of a teddy bear and ask him to point to the one in the bedroom. He is encouraged to name each of the objects if he is able. After he has matched each of the little pictures with the corresponding object in the bedroom scene, I put the little pictures which illustrate vocabulary that is familiar to him in front of the child and require him to hand me each one as I call for it.

7. **Introduce the concept of "middle".**

With the child watching I place three blocks in a row in front of the mother and say, "Mommy, give me the block in the middle." She complies. Then I remove the blocks and follow the same procedure first with stones and then with three cars. Now it is the child's turn. I place the blocks in front of him and say "Please give me the one in the middle." If he does not give the correct response, I show him what to do. We repeat the procedure with the stones and the cars. His mother is instructed to play the game at home with many different objects. When the child is able to respond correctly with groups of three, the same procedure is repeated using five and then seven objects. Later, he will be taught to follow directions such as "Here are some blocks. Put them in a row with the blue one in the middle."

8. Tell a story

Telling a story can be a very good way to finish a lesson. For this child I have chosen a book in which the plot can easily be followed through the pictures. Rather than read the text I tell the story myself using simple language that is familiar to the child. If it is a new story, he need only be a passive listener. If he has had the story on several previous occasions, he is encouraged to tell me as much of it as he is able. I hold the book in front of the child so that his eyes are directed to the pictures in front of him while he listens through his hearing aid to what I am saying.

In conclusion I would like to stress that **I firmly believe that to be most effective every teacher whether she be a mother or a professional person must find her own style.** I hope that some of my ideas will be helpful to the reader. However, they are in no way intended as rules to be strictly followed but rather as suggestions which might be tried.

Auditory training through daily routines

All your daily chores—preparing meals, making beds, cleaning, shopping, doing the laundry—are terrific opportunities for informal auditory training because children usually love to be involved in whatever mother is doing.

1. Auditory training in the kitchen

When you're **cleaning vegetables at the sink,** stand your child up on a chair beside you and let him clean vegetables too. While you are working right beside him, you can talk: "We're washing the carrots . . . Here's a carrot . . . Wash the carrot . . . The carrot's dirty . . . Wash the carrot some

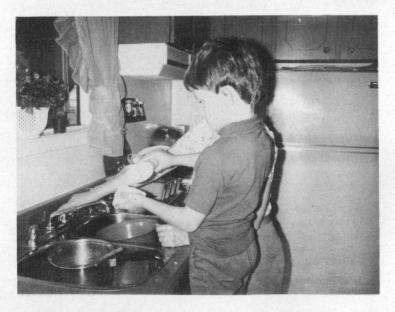

Helping with the dishes

more". Many children are happy to wash vegetables day after day for months and you can use this opportunity for teaching many words: *water, wash, dirty, clean,* as well as the names of fruit and vegetables.

Do the same thing when you're cutting up or peeling vegetables and fruit. Give him a carrot, or a potato, or a piece of celery and let him cut too. Let him make his own pot of vegetable soup as you make soup or his own casserole as you make one for dinner. He may never finish his casserole, but he'll get tremendous pleasure out of cutting and you'll have had a chance to stand close to him and review the names of the vegetables and many words and phrases such as "Cut it up"... "Put it in the pot", etc.

Baking, too, is excellent for informal language teaching. Many children love to mix different ingredients together, cracking open and beating eggs, rolling cookie dough into balls, etc. Most children, between the ages of one-and-a-half and three can't resist touching and messing with all the ingredients that go into cookies or a cake, so let them have their own mixing bowl and let them mess all they want as you work close beside them making the cookies and talking all the time; "We're making cookies ... mmm ... I love cookies ... Do you like cookies ... You're helping me make cookies... We're both making cookies."

One of the reasons baking and cooking are excellent for language development is that when the family later eats whatever was baked or cooked, *all the language you used while baking can be repeated.* For example, when you serve the cookies after dinner, make a production out of it: "Look at the cookies ... We made cookies today ... Mmm, the cookies taste good ... I love cookies ... etc." and the while family can talk about the cookies.

When you first begin auditory training, you may feel that your child does not hear you as you talk in the manner described above because he will not respond to what you say. Keep talking anyway. Imagine that he does hear it all. You really have no way of knowing how much of it he does hear; but it's better for him if you assume he does hear it all. Just like a normal infant, he has to soak up a great deal of language before his brain sorts it all out and he can begin using it himself.

Because you spend so much time in the kitchen, **keep pictures up on your kitchen walls.** One mother describes how this can be valuable:

"I always put pictures which illustrated lesson words on my kitchen wall (I used masking tape because it came off easily and didn't mark the wall). Frequently, when I sat down, my child would come to sit on my lap so I had a perfect opportunity to review a few words. I would ask her to point out the pictures—"Where's the man sleeping?" "Where's someone running?", etc. I always let her help me put the pictures up and take them down. This afforded another opportunity to review the words. She soon came to regard the pictures as very important. She would show them to her father when he came home; to her babysitters; to grandmother or anyone else who came to our house and on each occasion, the words were reinforced. (I had instructed everyone to pretend the pictures were very important and to ask her about them). As her language grew, the established ritual of putting up and taking down pictures reinforced many ideas and expressions such as "Put up", "Take down", "Where should we put it". After a couple of years I was using language such as "Where do you think we should put the picture of the tiger?" or "You decide where the picture of the leopard should go". By this time I was trying to teach her such concept words as "deciding", "thinking" and "choosing".

We have been doing auditory training now for four years and we still put pictures up on the kitchen walls. Now they are not related to lesson material; I just use them to give us something interesting or unusual to talk about. Very often she herself will find a picture and put it up on the wall and then talk about it from time to time with whoever happens to be around."

Another mother describes the value of a kitchen blackboard:

"We glued a piece of wallboard to the kitchen wall just above the baseboard and then painted it with blackboard paint. Its location was great for a small child and it was useful for drawing pictures at first and then later for printing words. Three years after its installation, the children still use it frequently and keep me company as I prepare meals. They often want to talk with me about what they are drawing."

One mother keeps plants in her kitchen and describes how they can be useful in language development:

"Plants *sprout, grow, bloom, die* and eventually you want your child to learn all of these words. Generally, children are fascinated by plants because they are living things and change from day to day. As the changes occur, you and your child can talk about them. The routine of watering plants is especially good when you are working on *water, pour, wet* and *dry.* Potting and repotting plants gives you a chance to work on "fill" and "soil" as well as the parts of a plant—*roots, stem* or *leaves.*"

2. Shopping trips

There are many ways to turn a shopping trip into a language building experience. When you're just beginning auditory training, trips to the supermarket give you a chance to reinforce the simple ideas "going bye bye", "We're going bye bye in the car" etc. As you shop, you can point out and talk about a few things that you have been working on in lessons such as apples, juice, cookies.

Occasionally, **you can make a shopping list by using pictures**

of a few things that you are trying to teach. Let the child help you make the list or at least have him around when you're making it to introduce the words. Then, when you arrive at the store before you get out of the car, take the list out of your purse and review the words before you go in. Then in the store, do each item on the list in turn, first showing the picture to your child and saying something like "Here's some bread ... We're going to buy bread ... Where's the bread?... Find the bread ..." Talk in this way as you walk up and down the aisles looking for the bread. Finally, of course you find the bread. "Here's the bread ... We found the bread ... Hurray!" Repeat the same procedure with the next item. Shopping takes a long time this way, and many people stare at you and think you're rather strange. Pay no attention! Your child is learning a great deal. On each shopping trip, he will understand more and more, until one day you'll simply be able to ask him, without the help of any pictures, for the bread and he'll point in the direction of the bakery counter. And some day, even when you don't want to buy bread, he'll point to it as you pass and ask "Do we need bread today?"

Use the process of putting the groceries on the cashier's counter to review the items you purchased again; and unpacking the groceries at home for the final review.

3. **Auditory training at meal time**

   a) Place four or five objects that your child is learning the names of in the centre of the table, but spaced out so that you can clearly point to any one of them. Then have each member of the family take a turn first closing their eyes and pointing to the object named. Teach the game by having one of the parents or an older brother or sister go first. For example, you may be teaching apple, banana, flower and cup. Place these on the table. Then say to your husband: "Daddy, close your eyes". After he has done so say "Where's the banana?" He should then point to the banana. When he does so, clap and smile and praise him very enthusiastically. He should look very pleased with himself (you really have to be a ham). Then someone else has a turn.

When your child is very young, hold him on your knee when you're going to play the game. Even if he does not want to participate, he will be close enough to you to hear all the language connected with the game.

Always use objects you have been working on in the lessons. This will encourage your child to participate in the game and to be successful most of the time.

b) Instead of sitting at the table, each member of the family in turn can go and stand, facing a wall near the table and then come back to the table and point to the object which was asked for.

c) When your child is learning action words, each member of the family in turn goes to the end of the room, turns his back towards the table, listens for the instruction and then performs the requested task. At first, the tasks are simple—"Jump", "Hop", "Sit down", "Stand up", etc. As the child's language grows, everyone is asked to do more complicated things—"Stand on the stool", "Stand beside the stool", "Get under the stool", for example, when you are concentrating on teaching him prepositions; or "Jump three times", "Jump two times", "Jump four times", etc. when he is learning to count.

When you are teaching him the names of shapes, draw the shapes on fairly large pieces of paper and place these on the floor at the end of the room. Each person in turn is then asked to "Jump on the triangle", "Jump on the square", "Jump on the circle", etc. Children love action games of this type.

d) This is a game to help the child associate the words "Mommy" and "Daddy" with his parents. The game can be played with just the child and two parents but it is more fun if other members of the family, or friends, can join in.

One parent stands beside the child at one end of the room. The other parent stands across the room facing away from them. If it is mother who remains with the child, she calls in a slightly louder-than-normal voice, "Daddy", and Daddy turns around. Then Mommy and Daddy exchange places.

When the child gets the idea and eventually learns to say these words, both parents can stand across the room while the child calls them and watches them turn around. The game can be expanded to teach the child the names of other people familiar to him.

e) Occasionally, announce towards the end of a meal that there is a surprise under everyone's plate. The surprise can be a picture of something. Then you can all talk about your picture. At the beginning the dialogue will be simple: "I have a car ... Do you have a car, Mommy?" ... "No, I have a rabbit ... Hop, hop, hop ... The rabbit goes hop, hop, hop", etc. As the child gets more language, the dialogue becomes more complex. For example, if the child has learned some colors, Daddy could say: "I have a blue car ... See my blue car ... I don't like blue ... It's not my favorite color ... (Obviously, he has to act disappointed. You have to be quite dramatic in all these games). My favorite color is yellow ... I love yellow ... I wish my car was yellow." At this point, Mommy can say: "I have a yellow cup" as she holds up her picture. "Here's a yellow cup ... But I wish mine were green ... Green is my favorite color ... Who has something green? ... Green is my favorite color". As you can see, the emphasis here is on the word "favorite". Parents should confer briefly before dinner for a game like this so that the words or ideas you want to concentrate on are appropriately emphasized.

f) This is not a game, but it is an idea one mother used which fits in here: She wrote:

"I have always used candles on the table at meal-time and this has given us many opportunities to review and reinforce language. At first, my child was fascinated by the candle and we used it to teach the word "candle" and other expressions such as "Blow it out", "It's hot", "Don't touch it", "Light the candle", "It's burning."

I frequently changed the color of the candle when we were learning colors.

We talked about "What's the candle made of?" when she was learning such concepts as "made of wood", "made of plastic", "made of paper", "made of metal". The ideas of "melting" and "dripping" were reinforced over and over again by our dinner table candles. I bought "long" candles and "short" candles, "fat" candles and "thin" candles to reinforce all of these concept words. Frequently, my husband would "forget" to light the candle at the beginning of a meal so that she could learn this word.

From time to time, we would run out of candles and I can remember using these occasions to teach "annoyed". My husband would pretend to be very "annoyed" because there was no candle on the table.

This year, I took her shopping before Chirstmas especially to buy candles and bought only red, green and white candles. She wanted to buy pink because that is her favorite color. But I used the occasion to teach her that red, green and white are Christmas colors. When Valentine's Day came, she wanted to know what the special Valentine's colors are and insisted that we have the appropriately colored candles. Right now, we are using candles to talk about the past: "Long ago, people didn't have electricity. They used candles to light their bedrooms, etc."

This demonstrates how one simple object, a candle, can

be a focal point of language development for several years.

g) Another mother wrote about how place mats can be used in much the same way as candles:

"When my child was two years old, I bought four brightly colored place mats made of durable vinyl plastic and having animal shapes. One was a white pig covered with large pink polka dots, one was a hippopotamus with yellow flowers all over his back, one was a yellow dog and the fourth one a red elephant. We have used these almost every night since I bought them three years ago. At first, they were terrific just for reviewing the animal names. As we ate we would talk about them: "Where's the elephant?", "Where's the hippopotamus?", etc. and everyone in the family could take a turn answering the questions.

After she learned the animal names, they were useful in teaching her "Mommy", "Daddy", and her own name. Every evening as we set the table, I would say "Who should have the elephant?" "Who should have the dog?", etc. She never answered because at this time she didn't talk much but she would take each mat and set it at some-one's place. As she did this, I would follow her around saying "Daddy has the elephant ... Daddy sits here", etc. Later as we ate, I would repeat the same language.

For example, I would say, "Daddy has the ele-phant", and he would smile and say something like, "Yes, I have the elephant". Eventually, she de-veloped a preference for one of the place mats and, at this point, I always gave each of us the same one every night and we talked about "your favorite" and such things as, "I like it best", or "I prefer it". Quite some time later, when she had developed a great deal of language, we reviewed such ideas as "real", and "unreal", with these place mats. "A real elephant is not red, it is grey", etc. Later, we related the animals to the characteristics of the persons in our family. For example, baby brother always had the pig place mat because he was, "messy, like a little pig, and always dropped food".

Place mats can be collected from restaurants and then used at home when you wish to talk about a recent family trip. When the child is very young, use them immediately the next day. However, as the child gets older you can use them a longer time after the trip. This will give you a chance to use language connected with the passing of time.

You and your child can make picture place mats for use at mealtimes. These can promote excellent table conversations.

4. Make the most of special occasions

Birthdays: It is important to plan something very special for your child's birthday party every year because over the years he will learn far more complex language than simply, *cake, candle, present,* etc. He will learn, each year as his birthday comes along that he is *growing up, getting older, getting taller,* etc. The time concept of "next year", can be reinforced with birthdays. Eventually, a great deal of comparative language gets reviewed and reinforced. "You are taller this year than you were last year", etc. Eventually, you can teach him such words as "plan" by letting him help you plan one of his parties in great detail: "How many people should we invite?" . . . "What shall we have to eat?" etc.

One mother explained that she always had a birthday cake, complete with candles and dinner guests, for the birthdays of all members of the family. This enables you to do a lot of comparing of the parties.

For all special events such as Hallowe'en, Christmas, Valentine's Day, Easter, etc., **introduce your child to the language associated with these events before they actually happen.** Then as the events occur, they are not only more meaningful to him, but you can review all the language again.

And talk about special events from time to time during the year. For example, take your Christmas Books out in July and read them with your child for review.

5. Family trips

Family trips provide an excellent opportunity for expanding the hearing handicapped child's vocabulary and relating it to the world around him. Trips to a park, to a cottage, to an airport, to a marina, to a movie, to a museum, to a zoo, even to a restaurant are invaluable in reinforcing the old vocabulary (which might have been acquired in a less stimulating learning situation, i.e. from pictures and books) as well as introducing new.

For example, when you are at the cottage you may suggest a walk in the woods. As you are walking you are, no doubt, going to encounter some interesting experiences:

"Look, there is a baby frog! ... Let's catch it! ... I got it! ... Here, you can hold the baby frog ... Don't squeeze it ... Hold it gently ... The baby frog feels cool ... It tickles your hand ... It's trying to get out ... Do you want to let it go free?"

You can catch grasshoppers, butterflies, snakes (if you're brave enough) and talk about these at great length. You can pick berries; you can pick flowers; you can collect leaves in the Fall, you can go for a picnic, you can gather wood for a bonfire and each time you have a variety of experiences to talk about. Different seasons of the year present different opportunities for your child to learn about nature in an enjoyable way.

Later the vocabulary and the experiences of the trips can be reinforced again by looking at the snapshots that you might have taken or by drawing pictures and short picture stories about the trips.

How does father fit in?

The fact that we have directed this book at mothers may create the impression that fathers do not need to get actively involved in auditory training. This, of course, is not true, but it is very difficult to say exactly what a father's role should be.

Every family embarking on auditory training should discuss the extra obligations placed on them by having to teach the child and decide how they will carry them out. Generally speaking, it will be the mother who will be organizing and carrying out the child's more formal language learning program.

Father helps build an engine

Most women, upon reflection, agree that it is quite unreasonable to expect a man who has been working under a great deal of stress all day to come home and do a language lesson. However, just because the child is deaf is no reason for father not carrying out his normal role—playing games, giving a bath, reading bedtime stores, enforcing discipline, etc.

At the beginning, however, a woman may feel resentment towards her husband because she has to do the lessons and her husband does not. Also, a husband may feel resentful that his wife seems to be devoting all her time to the child and leaving him last. Both parents must work very hard to keep the problem in perspective and also to avoid making the hearing impaired child the scapegoat for family problems.

The following are a few suggestions on how fathers can help:

a) Do not complain if the house is not perfectly neat and tidy. In the first couple of years of auditory training, mothers find themselves with little time for serious housework. When you are trying to take advantage of every opportunity for teaching your child, routine and organization are often impossible.

b) Be a good listener when mother feels like talking about the problem and be sympathetic when she feels like crying.

c) Give mother a break (even if it's only twenty minutes) by playing with or entertaining the child when you get home from work. She desperately needs this, particularly if the hearing impaired child is an only child and she has been alone with him all day.

d) Encourage her to get a babysitter to provide time, not only so she can get out by herself but also so that the two of you can regularly get out alone together, away from the child. Occasionally, a weekend babysitting exchange can be arranged with friends to give the two of you a chance to get away alone.

e) Participate enthusiastically in auditory training games.

f) Remember which words the child is learning in lessons each week and try to reinforce these casually as much as possible.

g) Be enthusiastic about the child's progress, no matter how slow, to make mother feel her efforts are worthwhile.

Father and son enjoy a story

Auditory training through books

All of us can remember being told to read books and stories to our children and to use books in our lessons and we can remember very vividly those first frustrating visits to children's bookstores. There we were faced with hundreds of books. "Which ones should I buy?" Many of us tended to go overboard and thought we had to buy everything. This, of course, is not necessary.

Having worked with our children for a few years, we have found that certain books are far more valuable than others for expanding a child's language and certain books appeal to children much more than others. And it is not necessary to buy every book you are going to use. Most communities have reasonably well-stocked public libraries.

The following gives suggestions about the kinds of books that will be useful with brief explanatory notes on how and when we used them.

1. Picture dictionaries

A couple of good ones are worth purchasing because you can use them as a source of lesson material for years. We would suggest:

a) *The Cat in the Hat,* by P.D. Eastman

This one will entertain your child for years because it is very funny. But its outstanding feature, from a language development point of view, is that it presents words in context and unlike the type of dictionary which simply names objects, presents pictures to illustrate many abstract words and ideas, e.g. words such as "almost", "going to", "hardly", "alone".

One mother bought two copies of this and cut them up for lesson pictures. She is still using these pictures in lessons after four years.

b) *Best Word Book Ever,* by Richard Scarry

This book also has delightful pictures and covers every subject from your home and what goes on in it to shopping, transportation, the circus, school, etc. Just about every subject you can think of can be introduced through this book.

c) *The New Golden Dictionary,* Golden Press, New York

This one has 1,712 words and over 2,000 pictures. This deals with abstract concepts as well as names of objects. As one mother said, "If I couldn't find a word in any other dictionary, I could always find it in this one."

d) There are many many inexpensive picture dictionaries (some cost less than $1.00 each) which are worth buying because you can cut them up and use them as a source of lesson pictures. Some of these are:

1. *Little Golden Picture Dictionary,* The Golden Press. This one can often be found in your local supermarket.

2. *500 Words to Grow On,* Random House, New York. This one would probably have to be ordered through a bookstore, but it's worth buying because it is very contemporary in the pictures it presents. Such things as hot dogs, hamburgers, power lawn mowers are included and the appliances, cars, buildings, etc. all look familiar to the child. A picture book with old-fashioned pictures is not as good initially as one with pictures which look exactly like the things the child sees.

3. *Golden Shape Books,* Golden Press. These are not really dictionaries, but we have included them here

because they do not tell stories but rather deal with one subject. *The Shopping Book* tells of all the places you go shopping and can be used when introducing words such as buying, selling. *The Sign Book* is excellent for talking about all the signs you may encounter as you go about with your child. There are many many books in this series—*The Sand Pail Book* which is great for summertime; *The Baby Book* is terrific if you are expecting a new baby in the family; *The Dinosaur Book, The Bunny Book, The Bird Book* are all excellent. These are very definitely worth what they cost.

2. Story books

Dictionaries are useful, but don't limit your child to them. Story books are just as important, perhaps more important in the long run for many reasons. They give your child's vocabulary and language a richness which no dictionary ever can. Through stories, your child will come to understand that the same words and expressions can be used in many different ways in many different situations. He will come to understand that there are many different ways to express the same idea. And stories will help your child with sequencing (i.e. putting things in order of first, second, third). But most important of all, stories will stimulate your child's imagination and encourage him to think. And they will entertain you as well as him. You may be surprised at how enjoyable children's literature really is!

Many mothers think they have to wait until their child has a great deal of language before they can introduce him to story books. And those who do begin to use story books quite early with their child often find it frustrating reading to a child who is not yet talking and reacting verbally to the story. You often wonder whether or not he hears you or whether or not he's getting anything out of it. The important thing to remember is: **the fact he is not talking does not mean that he is not listening.** So suffer through your own frustrations and make the stories as dramatic and interesting as you can. As long as he will sit and read with you, keep on reading. If he isn't getting anything out of it, he'll let you know quickly enough. He just won't sit there.

3. Simple stories for beginners

a) *Papa Small* by Lois Lenski. This book deals with family routines—father going to work, mother preparing dinner, cleaning the house, planting the garden, going shopping, etc. The pictures are clear, simple and very realistic. And the text also is simple. When you first begin, you can describe in your own words what is happening on each page; but this book is so simply written that you can soon read the text to your child exactly as it is written.

Other simple story books by the same author which are excellent are: *Spring Is Here; Now It's Summer; Now It's Fall; I Like Winter; Davey's Day; Animals For Me; The Little Farm; Policeman Small.* Most of these can be found in the children's section of the public library, so it is not necessary to buy them.

b) *Curious George,* by H.A. Rey. This is a favorite of all children but it is especially good for hearing impaired children because the pictures themselves really tell the story. Other books by the same author are: *Curious George Takes a Job; Curious George Rides a Bike; Curious George Flies a Kite.* Children love all of these from the time they are about 18 months old until they are five or six years old. Again, it is not necessary to buy them because they are available in most libraries.

c) *The Fierce Bad Rabbit,* by Beatrix Potter. This book has both simple pictures and very simple language. The pictures in all Beatrix Potter books delight young children, so you can use them even if the language in the stories is far too advanced for your child. Explain the pictures in your own words at a level you know he will understand. Again, the many stories of Beatrix Potter can be found in the library.

4. Nursery rhymes

Make no attempt to explain—the whole point is the rhythm.
Sing them too. Action ones are good to start with, e.g.
"This little piggy went to Market", using fingers and toes.
Bounce the child on your lap for "Ride a Cock Horse", or
"To market, to market, to buy a fat Pig".

5. Traditional children's stories

Apart from the fact that stories such as *The Three Pigs,
Goldilocks, The Three Billy Goats Gruff* are very much a
part of our culture (very few children in our country grow
up without knowing them), they are very important for
hearing impaired children because of the repetition of language patterns they contain. For example, in *Goldilocks,*
the pattern "Somebody's been ———— my ————" is repeated over and over again. It is the repetition of varied and
interesting language patterns such as are found in these
stories which will give your hearing impaired child's language richness and complexity.

Obviously, though, with a hearing impaired child you can't
read these stories just as they are written when you begin—
after all, you wouldn't read *Goldilocks and The Three Bears*
to a three, four, or even ten month old baby. A two year
old hearing impaired child who has just begun to wear an
aid and receive auditory training is not ready for this type
of story. But you can expose him to the story early and
through repeated exposure to it, build his language up to
the point where he is able to listen to and enjoy the whole
thing, just as it is written. Some mothers begin to use these
books quite early while others wait until the child's language is more developed and present the story in a more
conventional manner.

One mother describes how she introduced her child quite
early to stories.

> "I have chosen the story of *The Three Billy Goats
> Gruff,* with pictures by Marcia Brown, Harcourt,
> Brace and World.

When my child was just beginning (i.e. after we had been doing auditory training for about eight months), I sat her on my lap and talked about one or two things on each page in simple language, pointing to each thing on the page as I mentioned it moving along quite quickly so she would not become bored. For example, "Here's a goat . . . Here's another goat . . . See the sun . . . The sun is shining . . . Look at the tree . . . A tall tree", etc. At this point I was reading primarily to review a few words which she had been learning (goat, sun, tree). I repeated this three or four times over a three week period and then took the book back to the library.

A few months later, when we were working on words such as "eating" and "walking" in lessons, I took the book out again. This time as I read it, I said something like, "See the goats . . . The goats are eating grass . . . There's the troll . . . The troll likes to eat goats . . . The troll wants to eat the goat . . . Don't eat me, said the goat . . . O.K. I won't eat you, said the troll . . . Another goat is walking over the bridge . . . The troll wants to eat the goat . . . Don't eat me, said the goat . . . O.K. I won't eat you, said the troll, etc." Again I read fairly quickly so she would not get bored. Also I tried to read with a great deal of expression in my voice. Again, I did this two or three times in a three week period and took the book back to the library.

I took the book out again some months later when we were doing some counting. By this time, we had also been working on concepts such as "big" and "little". This time I read it like this: "Here are some Billy Goats . . . let's count them . . . one, two, three . . . the three goats like to eat grass . . . Which one is the big Billy Goat? Can you show me the big Billy Goat? . . . Here's the big troll . . . Isn't he big? . . . See his big nose and his big eyes . . . The big troll wants to eat the little goat ... Please don't eat me, says the little goat ... etc." By this time, I think my child was beginning to get some of the gist of the story.

Later, I took the book out when we were working on words such as "ugly", "wicked", "monster", and again for comparisons—"biggest", "smallest".

Eventually, by the time she was four and a half, I was able to read the story just as it was written so that she could hear the repetition of the language patterns. And the story, as written, was excellent for introducing words and phrases such as "gobble", "crush", "a tiny voice", "a gruff voice".

One of the reasons I chose *The Three Billy Goats Gruff* to write about, is that this year, in my child's kindergarten class, the teacher chose this story as the basis for a whole unit of work covering three or four weeks. The children made puppets and acted out the story, and my daughter was able to participate fully because she knew the story so well. The teacher later used the story of *Goldilocks* as the basis for a unit of work."

Among the many other children's stories which can be handled in this way are:

Henny Penny
The Gingerbread Boy
Jim and the Beanstalk (by Raymond Briggs. It is a somewhat modernized version of the traditional fairy tale Jack and the Beanstalk).
The Three Little Pigs
Too Much Noise by Ann McGovern, Houghton Mifflin Company.
Millions of Cats by Wanda Gag.

As well as nursery rhymes.

6. Books to develop the musical rhythmical qualities of your child's language

Some children's books are like poetry—they tell an extremely simple story, but the language in which the story is told is lilting and rhythmical, almost like music. Your child will enjoy listening to them, not at the beginning of auditory training, but later as he begins to put words together and his listening skills have improved. A few of these are:

Drummer Hoff. Adapted by Barbara Emberly, Prentice-Hall.

Pop Corn and Ma Goodness by Edna M. Preston, Viking Press.

Mommy, Buy me a China Doll by Harve Zemach, Follett Publishing Company.

When We Were Very Young by A.A. Milne.

7. Sensory and action books

These are books such as pop-up books, scratch and sniff books, touch and feel books. Generally, these books are not in public libraries and are expensive. But they can be useful for developing your child's sensory language. So keep a list handy for grandmothers and aunts who want suggestions for birthday and Christmas gifts. A few of these are:

a) *Pat the Bunny* by Dorothy Kunhardt. This is especially excellent for children between the ages of one and two.

b) *The Touch Me Book* (A Golden Touch and Feel Book). Young children enjoy the different things on the pages and as their language grows they can learn such words as *soft, furry, stretchy, scratchy.*

c) *In and Out Sesame Street Pop Up* (Random House). This vividly illustrates with pictures which the child can manipulate such concepts as *in* and *out*, *on* and *off*, *above* and *below*, *day* and *night*, *fat* and *thin*, *Yummy* and *Yucchy*, most of which you will be doing at some point in your lessons. Children enjoy this book from a very young age.

d) *The Sweet Smell of Christmas.* This is a scratch and sniff book which makes a wonderful Christmas gift, even for a two year old.

The books we have suggested are by no means the only ones you should use. We hope, however, these suggestions have given you some idea of the types of books you can use and different ways in which you can use them. One thing you should do if there is a public library in your community is go there by yourself occasionally to browse through the children's books and to familiarize yourself with children's literature. Become acquainted with the librarian too, and explain about how you are working with your child. She will always be glad to help and can usually put her hands on exactly what you want in a matter of seconds.

8. The library

Going to the library regularly with your child over the years becomes a wonderful language building experience. One mother explains how:

> The ideas of "borrowing" and "returning" things, "owning" things, "taking care of things that belong to others", "choosing books", "being allowed to take out a certain number of books", can be reinforced time and time again. You have to be quiet in the library because you "disturb" others if you're noisy. You have to "wait your turn" to check out books. I have taken my child to the library about once a month for the last three years. When we first went, she just wanted to throw all the books off the shelves and run around. The last time we went she said, "Are you pleased that I reminded you about going to the library?" Recently I have been using our trips to the library to teach her "remind me". I tell her every day for about a week before we go to "Remind me that we have to go to the library next week—on Tuesday."

*Choosing a
library book*

*Enjoying a story
with mother*

Auditory training can include nursery school

Sometimes parents are doubtful about sending their hearing impaired pre-school child to a nursery school (or pre-Kindergarten) with the local children. They feel perhaps that they are "cheating" because for some hours every day the child will not receive intensive auditory stimulation. Perhaps, since he is not speaking well enough to be understood by everybody, he will be thought of as stupid. Maybe the teacher will be upset by having a child who is "different", or the other children will reject him. Certainly, nobody could reasonably expect a school to alter its whole program just to suit one child.

This last reason is why it is such a very good idea to send him to nursery school. **It is a place where he has to learn how to behave just like any other child, that is, normally. He has to learn to make adjustments to the world sometime. It is much, much easier if he starts young, just like everyone else.**

As for fitting in and being backward in speaking, dealing with these two conditions are two of the things that a nursery school is geared for. Do not imagine that all the other children have perfect diction and fluent command of English, nor that they have perfect social poise! And as for rejecting, they are still at the completely self-centred stage of development where the peculiarities of others really do not interest them too much.

A teacher in nursery-age schools is very much aware that, in the early years at least, language achievement is only one aspect of progress in thinking. She will be looking for other signs of intelligence when evaluating your child. Some of the behaviors she will note are listed below. An example of each is given to clarify the meaning, but, of course, there would be hundreds of other examples for each child. Some suggestions for the types of language you could introduce are also given.

111

1. Can the child COMPARE AND CONTRAST? Does he know whether two blocks are the same or different? Can he indicate in what way they differ? Language here: colors, shapes, sizes, "the same", "different from", "bigger than", etc.

2. Can he SUMMARIZE? Can he pick out the important details of his day; a story he wants to tell you; a T.V. show; or does he get mixed up with unimportant detail? If he sees a group of pictures, can he tell you which ones don't belong? For this he needs language which describes the daily events of life, especially the time phrases which can help in such organization like "after lunch", "soon", and action words like "go", "hurt", "break".

3. Does he OBSERVE? It is surprising how many children do not really notice which is going on around them. Does he know where you keep the flour or other things he does not use himself? Accurate observation is a habit which has to be developed. His own experiences may give him no pressing need to look deeper. All sorts of "look" words come in here—and all sorts of "listen" ones, too. "What goes with . . .?" "Can you find any . . .?" "Did you see . . .?" "Where is . . .?" "Who said . . .?" "Was it really there?" "What else could we put in that picture?"

4. How does he CLASSIFY? Does he feel that some things go together? They may not be the same type of group that you would make but he should be able to give some underlying reason for his choice. Here is where all the attributive words come in: words such as "soft", "square" etc., and, of course, phrases indicating groups which "go together", "belong to".

5. He should be able to learn to INTERPRET or get meaning from a picture or a situation. He has to be guided not to assume more than the picture shows. For example, a picture of a crying child with a bleeding knee and a broken bike, makes it reasonable to assume that she fell off and hurt herself but not that a car ran into her. The last is only guessing and it is quite difficult for many children to realize

this. You help by working on "true" and "not true", "don't know", "guess", and do not worry that you are killing the child's imagination!

6. Another type of thinking is CRITICISM, making JUDGMENTS or EVALUATING. Listen to a pre-schooler, "I like ... I don't like ... That's stupid ... It's my favorite ... It's too ... It's not enough". These show a child beginning to realize that he too is a person with real ideas.

7. We all hold certain ASSUMPTIONS, or things we look on as certain: "Day follows night. There are clouds when it rains". These are based on our observations and experiments. The child has to make many trials and experience things many times before he makes assumptions, and no one can ever make them for him. He has to ask himself, "What would happen if ...?" "Which cup would hold more?" "Will this break if I throw it down?" "Will the cat scratch me if I pull its tail?" "How do you know that ...?" Some of these questions can be put to adults and save disaster, but only if he knows what to say. A useful word is "perhaps", and a phrase, "Shall we try to find out?"

8. Of course, all is not factual. Humans learn an enormous amount through play acting, pretending to be someone or something else. IMAGINATION leads to the understanding of the feelings of others and creates the need for vocabulary to express situations other than one's own "Let's pretend ——" "Tomorrow we will ——" (Because projection into the future is a kind of pretending too); "How does ... sound?" (remembering and recreating are also a sort of imagination); "Bad Teddy said, *I don't care!*" (using toys to work out little plays helps in antisocial behavior as well as vocabulary and teachers know that the ferocious whippings given to the bad guy do not really represent home life chez vous).

9. Just think how much time we save by our ability to COLLECT and ORGANIZE in everyday situations such as setting the table, getting ready to go out to play, going swimming. There is plenty of vocabulary here, e.g., "What do we need?" "I've forgotten something, I think". "Is that

everything?" "What else was there?" "Is that all?" And, of course, numbers.

10. One of the skills most needed in grade school is the ability to HYPOTHESIZE or make a theory. If you like, you could call it organized imagination. Teachers are always asking, "Why do you think the rabbit pricked up his ears?" "If I were going to the Arctic what would I take with me?" "Here the "If" is the big word. Also, of course, "Do you think", "I think so too", "no I don't think", and "perhaps", "maybe", "possibly".

11. Another thing the child has to learn to do is to learn from his mistakes and experiences and to build on what he already knows. He has to APPLY FACTS and PRINCIPLES in his daily life. It is a wise mother who says, "What would happen if you went out without your rubbers today?" She is giving him a chance to remember what happened last time they were caught in the rain and helping him to think. "Put on your rubbers" may have the same effect to her, but not to him.

When you are playing pretend games do not be in too much of a hurry to show how much you know. "What could we use for a cup?" is much better than, "Let's use a leaf for a cup". He is the one then who is thinking of the basic characteristics of a cup.

12. Even little children have to MAKE DECISIONS. You can help by limiting the available choices to his ability to manage the problem. "Would you prefer an orange or a brown popsicle?" rather than, "What flavor of popsicle would you like?" Help him to stick to his choice, too. "Well, that's too bad. Next time you'll know to choose an orange one."

13. How is your child as an INVESTIGATOR? Does he set about finding out something in an intelligent way by using his powers of observation, asking questions and then applying what he knows? Is he the kind who pulls a chair over and then climbs up, finishing by "making cocoa" all

over the clean kitchen floor? Never mind, he is trying to *find out* for *himself.* Anyway, think of the chances of language as you are close together mopping it up!

All the question forms are needed for finding out. Also phrases like, "Let's find out." "Who would know?" "Let's go the the Library." ". . . could tell you." "Go and ask Daddy." "Try it and see."

The report which you get from the nursery school will list various social and intellectual skills. The teacher has watched your child as he performs in the group, to see how he compares with others and how he matures in himself. You can see there are plenty of things for her to notice besides facility in language.

The purpose of the nursery school is to provide a place where all these desirable types of thinking can be encouraged, as well as introducing a child to ways of getting along with others.

In nursery school with normal children, the hearing impaired child learns from the rest of the group all the time.

You will notice that your child, like all the others, is learning from the rest of the group all the time. He will learn to act as they do—including saying things which no adult ever teaches him, like, "Stupid idiot". Do not expect this to happen right away. It will have to mature a little. Just wait until the summer holidays and you will probably be surprised, delighted and shocked by the amount of language that your child has picked up from his environment. Here is when you get proof that the auditory training has worked.

Of course, there are other bonuses for you in nursery school. At last you have a quiet time to organize your lessons, your meals and yourself. There is time to share with the rest of the family. Try never to forget that the hearing impaired one is only PART of the family, not the whole thing. At the least he has parents, possibly also brothers and sisters. Every one of them needs attention and fun (Yes, even Mom as well!).

The school can be a great help to you in lesson planning. Perhaps you may get a chance to spend a few hours helping with the class. Certainly, you can find excuses to pick your child up from time to time. Watch and listen. What are the other children of his age doing and thinking and saying? Use these observations to gear your lessons to his real interests.

Best of all, there is the teacher. Here, at last, is a colleague. She knows your child and is interested in his progress. She is trained in the handling of small children. To her he is an exciting challenge—but still basically a child with skills and problems like the rest. She will be delighted and flattered if you ask her for help and advice. You will find, possibly to your astonishment, that your problems are not so different after all. He acts that way because he is four—not because he has a hearing impairment.

Part III

An audiogram

what does it mean?

Hearing aids

success depends on good aids

keeping the aid in good working order

Pure-tone audiogram

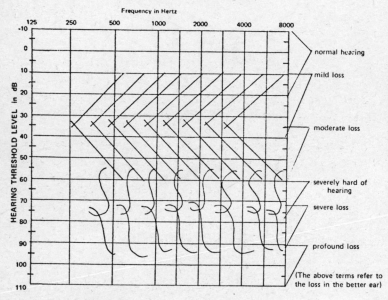

normal hearing

mild loss

moderate loss

severely hard of hearing

severe loss

profound loss

(The above terms refer to the loss in the better ear)

SPEECH AUDIOMETRY

Speech Discrimination — Percentage of words recognized correctly.
Speech Awareness Threshold (SAT) — Speech sounds can be just heard.
Speech Reception Threshold (SRT) — Speech can be recognized.

Pure Tone Average is calculated on the average of the responses to 500, 1,000 and 2,000 Hz. The patient is said to have a loss of — dbs.

"difference in dB"		AUDIOGRAM CODE					
		AIR		BONE		Free Field F.M.	Sta-pedial Reflex
Color	Ear	Un-masked	Masked	Un-masked	Masked		
Red	R	O –O	Δ–Δ	⊐··⊐	>··>	✳	R
Blue	L	X–X	☐–☐	⊏··⊏	<··<		Я
		⊏⊐ : Bone Vibrator on ___ Mastoid					

118

An audiogram -What does it mean?

Before your child was diagnosed as having a hearing problem you and he had probably gone through a lot of testing. You may even have been given or shown a chart called an audiogram, and, like many parents, you have no idea what it means.

In very simple terms, the audiogram is a chart which shows how much louder than normal a sound has to be at each frequency before your child will respond to it. The loudness of the sound is plotted up and down on the graph in units called decibels. The frequency, or pitch, of sound is recorded across the audiogram in units called Hertz (Hz) per second. (The old name for Hertz was cycles per second and you sometimes still see cps.)

To understand what frequency means, think of a guitar string. Stretch it out and pluck it. It will give a lowish sound and will vibrate a certain number of times during a second— cycles per second. Stretch it tighter and tighter and the sound gets higher and higher and the vibrations faster and faster. The greater number of cycles per second, the higher the sound. The range for human speech is considered to be 300-3,000 Hz, although speech sounds are actually perceived over a very much wider range.

To understand "decibels", imagine that we have several whistles each tuned to a different frequency and some way of measuring how much air we need to blow them (rather like the dial which shows pressure when you pump up a car tire). First we find out how much blow is needed for the average person to hear the tiniest sound in each pipe and plot that on the graph. This we could call the line of normal hearing, marked '0' on the audiogram. Each pipe could then be blown louder and louder until it became intolerable, painful to hear. This would be the limit at which the average person could stand sound (threshold of pain). It is 140 decibels and not generally shown on the audiogram at all. After all, it would hardly do to hurt people when you were testing them.

The fact that sound can be too loud for human beings to tolerate limits the amount of amplification possible in a hearing aid. You obviously cannot just make all sounds louder when it might hurt the wearer. In fact, exposure over sometime to very loud sounds will certainly hurt your hearing.

If you still feel that you are a bit shaky on decibels we suggest that you write to:

Fisher Controls Company of Canada,
Woodstock, Ontario.

for their free 16-page programmed booklet, "Understanding Decibels."

When a child is tested, he is presented with sounds at the different frequencies (250, 500, 1,000 etc.) and the loudness or decibel level at which he begins to hear each frequency is marked on the chart. When all the frequencies have been tested, the findings are joined in a graph. This line shows where your child begins to hear; it is called his hearing threshold. The space between that line and the bottom of the audiogram plus a bit extra, not shown on the chart, represents the area in which he can hear sound. If a loss of 60 dbs. was shown evenly across his audiogram, sound would have to be amplified to 60 dbs. louder than normal before he would start to hear it.

Seldom, if ever, does anyone lose their hearing evenly; that is, with an equal loss in all frequencies. Actual amplification in a hearing aid has to try to match uneven losses, while at the same time remembering that some sounds are more important for speech and others tend to blot out weaker sounds. This is one of the reasons why it is important to have your child tested and his aid fitted by a qualified audiologist who is trained to take such considerations into account.

The most important thing to remember about your child's audiogram is that it does not mean very much in terms of what your child can or cannot do after he begins to wear a hearing aid and to receive intensive auditory training, either at home or in a clinical or school program. Some children whose audiograms are in the profound range (80-110 dbs.) learn to function as merely hard of hearing because they learn to use their residual hearing so well, while other children whose audiograms show a severe loss (60-80 dbs.) sometimes develop very little useful hearing.

All that an audiogram really says about any child, and particularly any infant, is that he is behaving abnormally in the presence of sound stimuli. It does not tell how that child will behave with amplification and auditory training. **So do not make predictions about your child's future on the basis of his audiogram.**

Do not despair if you have been told that it was impossible to get an audiogram of your child, or even a response. Over the years, many parents have had this experience and nearly every one thought that this meant that their child was 'stone deaf', i.e. no hearing at all. This, of course, is utter nonsense.

Little children are extremely difficult to test. Testing by conventional methods needs both attention and realization of what sound is. American pure tone audiometers (the machines used for testing) stop at least 20 decibels short of the possible limit of usable hearing.

Of course, a great deal of research has gone on into finding some way of testing infants because we all want to know as soon as possible, more or less, what their loss is. Much has been discovered about reactions to sound at various ages and a good, experienced audiologist can make pretty accurate estimations but so far no one can honestly say that there is any infallible test of an infant's ability to hear.

Once a child gets a little older, especially if he has had some experience in listening, then he can respond in a meaningful way to the different types of tests and some real idea of the

Typical sound levels

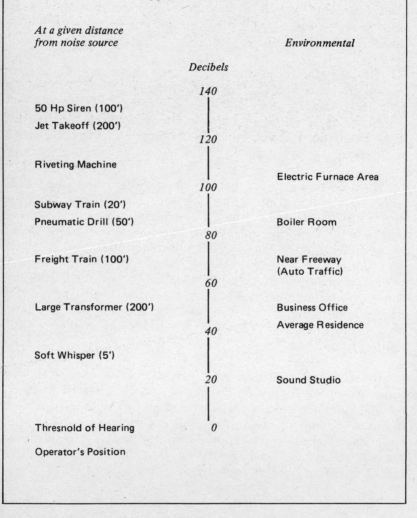

At a given distance from noise source	Decibels	Environmental
	140	
50 Hp Siren (100')		
Jet Takeoff (200')		
	120	
Riveting Machine		
		Electric Furnace Area
	100	
Subway Train (20')		
Pneumatic Drill (50')		Boiler Room
	80	
Freight Train (100')		Near Freeway (Auto Traffic)
	60	
Large Transformer (200')		Business Office
		Average Residence
	40	
Soft Whisper (5')		
	20	Sound Studio
Thresnold of Hearing	0	
Operator's Position		

extent of loss can be determined.

Never wait until that time. If your child should turn out to have normal hearing, no harm whatever has been done to him by auditory training, quite the contrary. The main thing to remember is that very, very few children turn out to have absolutely no hearing. Some researchers go so far as to say none. Even the most pessimistic admit that not more than seven per cent in schools for the deaf give no response and, of course, this may merely mean that they have not had a chance to learn how to listen.

Just make sure that your child's hearing has been tested by a qualified audiologist, not just a hearing aid dealer. And make sure that your child has been fitted with the type of hearing aid, or aids, that the qualified audiologist has prescribed.

TESTS FOR HEARING IN CHILDREN

INFORMAL TESTS: Sounds, either voice, noise makers or pure tones are given at different loudnesses while the child is playing. The responses are observed and evaluated.

FORMAL TESTS: The child is taught to make some sort of consistent response to sounds, either given in a small room or through headphones.

ELECTROPHYSIOLOGICAL TESTS: The child has electrodes attached to him and the conditioned or involuntary responses to sound are recorded and assessed by machine. P.G.S.R. records changes in skin resistance ('lie detector type'), while the E.E.R. (cortical) records electrical brain signals. Cardiotachometer measures heart rate change.

PURE TONE AUDIOMETRY: Refers to the sounds used as stimuli which are tones at different frequencies in the speech range. Pure tones do not occur naturally in speech or the environment.

VOICE AUDIOMETRY: (Speech Audiometry: Monitored Live Voice). The tester speaks in the machine which delivers the speech at a pre-determined loudness. A tape may be used.

AIDED TESTING: Either speech or pure tone testing with the hearing aid being worn.

AIR CONDUCTION: The sound is transmitted to the ear in the normal way.

BONE CONDUCTION: The sound is transmitted through the bones of the skull.

Hearing aids

Success depends on good aids

Your child's hearing aid is precious to him—it is his lifeline to the world of sound. We cannot emphasize its importance strongly enough. **The auditory training you do with him will be effective only if he wears his hearing aid or aids all his waking hours and if his aid is in perfect working order at all times.**

So, right from the first day your child has his aid, **make him understand that it is not a toy but rather something to help him hear.** Do not allow him to play with his aid, or chew it or bang it about. Do not allow him to put it on or off as he wishes or to play with the switches or volume control. Make it clear to your child right from the beginning that his aid is a delicate, sensitive machine which must be treated carefully.

With a young child this is easier said than done. Especially at first, he will be curious about his aid; he may insist on taking out his earmoulds hundreds of times a day. You may have to struggle with him to get it on at all. **You simply have to be firm and consistent in handling him.** He will soon learn to leave it alone and will accept that he must wear it, just as he accepts the fact that he wears a shirt or shoes.

Figure 1 is a drawing of a typical body type hearing aid. Very simply, the sound enters the aid through the microphone, is amplified and then carried to the ear by the receiver. When an aid is prescribed for your child by a qualified audiologist, he will also prescribe the volume and tone setting at which your child should wear his aid. **Be certain that it is set at the prescribed setting at all times.**

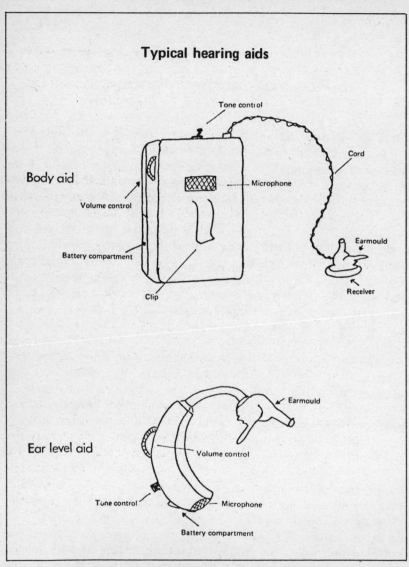

Typical hearing aids

Body aid

- Tone control
- Cord
- Microphone
- Volume control
- Earmould
- Battery compartment
- Receiver
- Clip

Ear level aid

- Earmould
- Volume control
- Tone control
- Microphone
- Battery compartment

Fig. 2

Keeping the aid in good working order

1. Batteries

a) Always make sure you buy the specific size of battery required by your child's aid. It does not matter what brand you buy (Zenith, Mallory, etc.) but the size must be the right one for your child's hearing aid.

b) Do not force the battery into the aid. If it is the correct size it will slip in easily.

c) Make sure when inserting the battery that the positive (+) sign on the battery matches the positive (+) sign on the aid. If the (+) signs do not match, the aid will not work.

d) Always test a battery, even a new one, before putting it in the aid because you cannot be sure the batteries you are purchasing are fresh. They may have lost some of their power just sitting a long time on a store shelf.

e) Buy a battery tester, because the batteries in your child's aid should be tested daily. You never know when the battery will lose its power.

f) Do not wait until the battery is completely dead before you change it. If a 1.4-volt battery is required for your child's aid, the aid will work best when the power of the battery is at 1.4. Once the power of the aid drops below 1.29, the aid will not be working at full power and your child will not be getting the most benefit from it. A battery should be discarded, then, when its power drops.

g) Once batteries have been purchased, store them in a cool, dry place. Be especially careful of moisture affecting both the batteries and the aid if you live in a very humid climate or if you are on a camping trip in the summer. One way to keep the batteries and aid dry under such circumstances is to store them in air-tight plastic bags along with a drying material which absorbs moisture; e.g. a piece of cheese-cloth full of rice. Some hearing aid dealers sell special Dry-Aid kits designed for this purpose.

2. Check the aid by listening to it daily

Follow the steps below when listening to the aid:

a) Set 1. the 'on-off' switch to 'off'
   2. the volume control setting on the lowest setting
   3. the 'tel-mic' switch to 'mic'
   4. the tone control to the setting most frequently used

b) Put the receiver in your ear and cover it with the palm of your hand. Hold the aid away from your ear to prevent feedback (whistling).

c) Turn the aid on, turning the volume control wheel up and down slowly, listening for scratchiness or dead spots. The volume control should not be too loose or too tight.

d) Turn the 'on-off' switch back and forth to check for intermittent sound or loose contacts.

e) Change the tone control switch to different settings, and listen for appropriate changes in pitch or quality of sound.

f) Roll the cord back and forth between your fingers and listen for 'cut-outs' of the sound. If the sound cuts on and off, the cord should be replaced.

g) Check the cord connections for firmness of contact at both the body of the aid and the receiver.

h) Tap the aid on all sides to check for reduced power or loose connections.

i) Check for loose screws on the case.

j) If the aid does cut on and off, is intermittently weak and strong and the problem is not eliminated by fresh batteries or a new cord, then return it to your dealer for service.

k) At your next appointment with the audiologist, ask him to review with you the procedure for listening to the aid. It is a good idea to listen to it yourself in his presence, so you can hear what the aid sounds like when it is functioning properly. Discuss what you hear with the audiologist in order to make you more aware of any breakdowns or abnormalities in its performance.

l) Make sure your child's aid has been tested by a qualified audiologist on B. & K. type equipment to ensure it meets the manufacturer's specifications for that type of aid. Do not be content to simply accept a dealer's assurance that, "It's a good aid". The child's aid should be tested at least once every six months routinely and should also be tested if the aid has been dropped or banged about unusually hard, or if it has fallen into water, or suffered some other mishap.

3. Feedback

This is the whistling sound which drives most mothers crazy. One of the main reasons it bothered me a great deal was because I knew when my child's hearing aid was feeding back, she could not hear anything. Once we had committed ourselves to an auditory approach, we wanted her to hear as much as she possibly could all the time she was awake. A child loses a great deal of auditory stimulation if the aid is feeding back most of the time.

With children, of course, there is bound to be feedback frequently during the day. For example, when they tug on their cords, even gently, the mould is loosened and the whistling begins. Almost every time they brush against something, run into something, jump about, wrestle, roll around, the mould is loosened. In these instances, you simply have to fit it back in tightly. Eventually, you can teach him to do this himself.

If feedback exists, however, when you have just fitted in the mould and your child is sitting still, it is probably caused by a poorly-fitting earmould. The process of making earmoulds seems to be very inexact and haphazard, and the only solution to the problem of feedback caused by a poorly fitting mould is to have it remade again and again until it finally fits. You have to be very aggressive about this and insist that the earmould be remade if it does not fit. Do not be satisfied to turn the volume of the aid lower than the setting prescribed for your child by the audiologist because of feedback. Do not move the aid too low down on the child's chest to avoid feedback, because when you do this, he does not get the best possible amplification of his own voice. Insist that a better fitting mould be made. This can often be a frustrating experience for both parent and child (one child I know of recently had to have a mould remade 12 times before it finally fitted properly), but it seems to be the only thing you can do.

Mothers from time to time come up with somewhat ingenious but temporary solutions to the feedback problem. For example, one mother said that her child's aid stopped feeding back if she put Nivea cream around the canal of the mould to act as a sealer. Another mother made a special hat with earflaps out of a light cotton fabric to hold the moulds securely in her child's ear.

A poorly fitting mould, while the most common cause of feedback, is not the only one. Before an earmould is remade, the aid should be checked as follows:

a) With the aid turned off and the receiver out of the ear, place your thumb firmly over the opening of the receiver. Turn the aid on with the volume all the way up. Listen for a soft whistling sound from the hearing aid case or receiver. The aid needs professional servicing if whistling is present internally.

b) Clean the earmould and attach it to the receiver. Place the thumb over the hole in the canal of the earmould and turn the aid to its loudest position. If you hear whistling at the receiver, be sure there is a plastic washer between the receiver and earmould. Re-check for whistling. If the feedback persists, return the aid to your dealer for service.

4. Care of the hearing aid

a) **Never get the body of the aid wet.** If your child is playing with water or anything liquid or messy, make sure he is wearing an apron to protect his aid.

b) Take special precaution to prevent juice, syrup, peanut-butter, cookie crumbs, soup, etc. from falling on the aid.

c) The earmould should be cleaned daily with water and soap. **Do not use alcohol or any other types of cleaners. Use only warm water and soap.** Use a pipe cleaner to clean the hollow parts.

d) To protect your child from infection, keep the ear clean. It will tend to secrete more wax because there is a foreign body (the earmould) in the ear canal. Ask your doctor how to keep your child's ears clean and free of wax because dreadful damage can be done by improper cleaning.

e) When the aid is not being used, store it at room temperature since extremely hot or cold temperatures will affect it.

f) Store the aid in a safe place so that it is not accidentally dropped, sat on, stepped on or knocked down.

5. Wearing the aid

A very important factor in language development is the child's ability to hear himself. Therefore, a child wears his

*Patch pockets
sewn on outside
of clothing*

*A leather harness
worn over clothing*

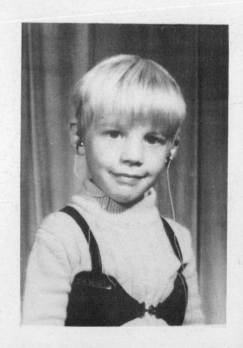

body aid on his chest in such a position that the microphone is close enough to the child's mouth to clearly amplify all his babbling and other attempts at vocalization.

Young children generally wear their aids in harnesses—either purchased from a hearing aid dealer or made by their mothers. Many mothers sew small patch pockets on the outside of the child's clothing to hold his aid.

All the children described in this book have always worn their aids outside their clothing (except outer wear such as coats and snowsuits) so that the microphones would be completely exposed and the noise from rubbing clothing eliminated. They feel that the children get the best possible amplification in this way. The child hears his own voice more clearly, too, if his microphone is uncovered.

Some of these mothers have also insisted that the hearing aid pocket be an actual part of whatever garment the child is wearing. As one mother explained in her story: "If we wanted people to talk to our child and to treat him normally, the paraphernalia of deafness had to disappear."

The photographs show several different ways that hearing

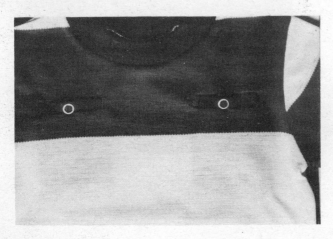

Concealed pockets sewn as the pockets of a man's suit

aids can be worn. Whatever type of harness or pocket you choose for your child, just remember that the harness, while allowing the child some flexibility for breathing, should fit tightly to the body, and that pockets should fit the aid snugly. An aid which bounces around on a child's chest loosely, day after day, is not going to remain in good working order very long.

6. Do not be afraid to ask questions

If there is any aspect of your child's hearing aid and its operation which you do not understand, **do not be afraid to ask your audiologist about it.** Write down the questions which arise as you and your child adjust to the aid so that at your next appointment with the audiologist, you will not forget to ask them. Write down his answers too! He understands that your child will be helped only if you understand how to help him, and will be happy to answer any questions and explain anything which is confusing you.

Part IV

In summary

a teacher listened, too

a mother's pledge

In summary
-A teacher
listened, too

"Doesn't hear" is not "Can't hear"

by Dorothy Scott.

For generations now, teachers have advised parents of young deaf children, "Talk, talk, talk." Parents have naturally asked, "What shall we talk about?" To which the traditional answer was, "Anything and everything."

So the parents went back home and said, "Ball" or "Cat", or "Drink" in appropriate situations, making quite sure that the child was watching and paying attention; and because children really are terribly clever at learning, a few actually did develop some facility in language. But really there had been a failure in communication between teacher and parent right from the beginning. The teacher meant the parents to talk as they would to any child, assuming that he can hear, in phrases and sentences; the parents, thinking of the kind of speech that infants produce, that is, one or two word expressions, tried to help their baby by limiting what they said to him.

The teacher knew that if you want real, natural language you must somehow get the child to go through all the same processes which a normal baby does. He lies there, watching and associating, soaking in all the mass of chatter. His method is one of trial and error. It is self-correcting. He picks out small sound groups and makes deductions BY HIMSELF. He is learning to think and understand long before he speaks. Then, after some months, or even years, he proudly says, "Ball."

This simple utterance required an enormous amount of experience. A normal baby's talk, when it comes, is merely the tip of the iceberg. He knows much, much more about language than the few words we hear.

But when it is your own baby, it is very hard to wait. Perhaps the method may never work? All your relatives seem to know of deaf children who talked instantly. Couldn't you just teach him to say, "Mama" or "Daddy"?

The teacher also knew that you CAN teach lanaguage, of a sort, by presenting structured and visible patterns. We all do it to a certain extent. "What do you say when Grandma gives you a cookie?" This is obviously rather limited and really a matter of form, for we have no guarantee that gratitude is what the child is feeling. He probably would prefer to say that he would like two.

Imposed, structured language cannot cover every situation. It is limited because you cannot use the word patterns very flexibly and it does not give the child the chance to develop normal thought processes. It is, in fact, second best.

Remember that *all* parents, naturally, unconsciously and effortlessly, teach their babies to talk, just as their parents taught them. The difference is that you, the parent of the hearing impaired child, are usually faced with an infant in hearing and a toddler in interest. Unless you were very lucky indeed, and your child was diagnosed very early you know that this is no passive baby. It is quicksilver in boots, it is curiosity, active.

So you think, "All very fine for you to talk, teacher, in your nice enclosed classroom from nine until three-thirty. I am competing with the whole world full of fascinating things. Every minute is valuable. What I say must help my child to understand his world fully . . . and I get so tired. And he never says anything, not real words." Such feelings make some people want to give up.

The parents who compiled this book have found a way which really works. They are sharing with us some of the exercises which they have found particularly valuable for their children. As a teacher, I feel very honored to be asked to add some of my comments. Unfortunately for my professional ego, I cannot claim that any of these children were my pupils. Many, indeed, will never need tuition from a teacher of the deaf; for a teacher of the deaf, this is a life-long dream come true.

Sometimes these parents (yes, even they!) wonder whether all their work was indeed necessary or whether their children would have learned to talk anyway. Let me assure them that there would be no possibility of this. Such deaf children could not learn to talk alone.

As a convert to auditory approaches to the education of hearing impaired children, I am overjoyed that so many small people are achieving so much in hearing and language in such a natural way. It is basically simple, for you act as you would towards any of your other children, except that you keep within the "Magic Circle" of the hearing range, i.e. close to the child's aid.

Why then, since it is so simple and since it really works, did people not do this before? How come that all teachers of the deaf are not sold on this approach?

Remember that simple does not necessarily mean easy and that many teachers work in a residential school situation. Realize that 25 years ago hearing aids were two rather large and weighty components; that there were no audiologists, only testers.

Let's go way back then. The testers had noticed that infant Tommy and old Uncle Joe might have the same hearing loss but very different responses to sound. Tommy ignored it, understood nothing said; Uncle Joe managed fine if you got near enough, didn't shout and spoke clearly. Even in those dark ages they had come up with the right answer. Joe had the experience and could fill in the gaps; just as we can visually when we see the sentence. "Th— c—t —s bl—ck." Whereas poor Tommy was like the non-Latin scholar faced with, "F—l—s n—g—r—st."

Most teachers started working with amplification. Nearly all classes got group auditory trainers and nearly all teachers used them some of the time. (They also had a practically permanent 'out of order' sign for them.)

Some people had tremendous success but the average class did not do too well. Certainly, some children learned to recognize a few words and, once nice little aids were available, quite a few suddenly improved beyond all expectation so that some were able to continue their education in normal classrooms. The average really deaf child did not generally improve enough to make up for the time taken from language training and school information subjects. The successes reported were usually individual parents working alone with their child, perhaps helped by an audiologist, teacher or speech therapist.

These children were shown proudly at conventions. But we all know how hard it is to diagnose the amount of hearing a young child has. He is, after all, mostly being asked to describe what he hears when he does not know what sound is. Faced with the successful one, teachers would compare him with their own pupils and say, "Well, he probably is only hard of hearing", or, "Look at his parents, the kid is certainly brilliant". And they think of their own classes—children of different ethnic backgrounds; children with multiple problems and poor home environments and give up the idea. A phrase, "Functionally hard of hearing", was coined to describe the child who acts as though he hears, although by his audiogram he should be deaf.

Should be deaf? Yes, the doctor and the audiologist said he was deaf—that means he cannot hear, doesn't it? So, we 'help' the poor afflicted child by making everything VERY CLEAR and pretty soon we teach him to be dumb in both senses of the word.

You see, nearly all of us forgot that Tommy was not Uncle Joe. We expected him to know all about hearing and to be able to tell us what he heard as if he were the old man who knew all about hearing before he developed his loss. All children, no matter how perfect their hearing, have to learn to listen. At first all they can do is jump and cry at sudden loud noises and cut off sounds which don't seem to them to have any particular meaning. Of course, with hearing impairment, there are an awful lot of such sounds. But every child has to have listening experiences or he will not learn to talk normally. Indeed, we still sometimes get the children of signing deaf persons in schools for the deaf who turn out really to have normal hearing. Without stimulus, their skills have never developed.

Learning to listen is going to take a good long time. As we said before, babies lie there thinking about speech long before they talk.

If your doctor had said, "He has a weak ankle", you would expect to do exercises for quite a while before baby could walk, and you would hardly expect a figure-skating champion at three. So when you have been told, in effect, "He has some malfunction in the auditory mechanism," **WHICH IS ALL ANYBODY REALLY KNOWS**, it is rather unrealistic, although human, to expect him to say, "Mama", after his first lesson. Indeed, the first utterances of the child who has been taught to listen will be, and should be imperfect. Like the normal child, he will vocalize, play with sounds, babble, use jargon and speak unintelligibly at first. Like the normal child, as his listening skills improve, so will his speech.

Can such training be done in a school for the deaf? Only if the teacher is truly able to work individually with each child and his exposure to other 'deaf' children is kept to the minimum. Remember that these children need even more experience in speech patterns than do normal children to make up for time lost and the deficiencies of their hearing. Like any other children, the more the situation fits their own particular stage of development, the more likely they are to learn from it.

Don't forget that by the time most children have reached school age, they will have worked out some form of communication for themselves. They haven't lived in a vacuum for five years. Even a six-year old is going to be reluctant to abandon his own inventions, particularly when they work. And even a six-year old is going to go along with the gang and use their method of communication, no matter what the teacher says.

So . . . it is long. It is hard work and time consuming. At the very least, the parents must be prepared to reinforce; often to do it all. But it is more worth the effort than you can possibly imagine.

A mother's pledge

1. I accept that more than anything else I care about the future of my hearing impaired child.

2. I accept the fact that nobody else is going to do the necessary work or make the necessary effort for me. I MUST do it myself.

3. I accept the fact that it is going to be difficult, perhaps the most difficult thing I have ever had to do.

4. I will seek help wherever and from whomever I need it; be it educational guidance, psychiatric counselling, audiological and medical advice or support from other parents. I will not be overawed by professionals; their services are available to help me.

5. **I will not let any "if onlys" get in my way.**
   "If only I didn't have younger children; if only I were wealthy; if only I had live-in help; if only I didn't have to work; if only my husband understood; if only by child had a little more hearing", etc.

6. I will not dwell unduly on the sacrifices which I am making.

7. I will always remember that any procrastination on my part now will threaten the future of my child.

8. I will organize my day in order to give myself sometime of complete privacy.

9. I will work hard and consistently and take a regular holiday.

10. I will have a good cry and ventilate my feelings without feeling ashamed.

11. When I am coping and my child is on his feet, I will return the help given to me by others for the benefit of other hearing impaired children and their parents.

Good luck and think positively.

Sally Farr
President: Voice for
Hearing Impaired Children

Part V

Five years later

The children

Auditory Training

- A teacher's update
- Lessons with older children
- Using the telephone
- Parents, be aware!

Hearing Aids Today

Jonathan

Jonathan is now nine-and-a-half years old and is in grade four in a split grade four/five class at his local public school. Jonathan has a five-year-old brother and a two-year-old sister, both with normal hearing. Jonathan has recently been fitted with ear level aids and is presently trying out a personalized FM unit during school hours. His unaided audiogram still shows a profound loss averaging 110 db, but after eight years of auditory training he continues to be an integrated child.

Our journey has turned into an incredible adventure. We set out eight years ago to prepare Jonathan for full participation in society. To help Jonathan reach his potential as an independent being in the mainstream meant creating a constant and consistent auditory environment for him. Then, as now, our options seemed crystal clear. We could look at our one year old in terms of his deafness, and through his pair of malfunctioning ears see all the things that he could never do; or we could look at this same infant and decide that we were going to educate a child with a mind, instead of a pair of ears. We decided **we would stop assuming all the things we thought he couldn't do and give him the opportunity to go just as far as he himself might be able to go.** Far from denying his deafness, we were prepared to deal with it. Deafness was **one** permanent part of his life, and although he never was and never will be the same as a normally hearing child, his feelings of worth and achievement were not related to and dependent on his sameness with those around him.

Auditory training helped us create a normal environment in which the development of speech and language followed the normal sequential development of any child. All models for speech and language, as well as for behavior, came from our normal environment. Jonathan was surrounded by people who believed that with his hearing aids on he could indeed hear. Every time we called his name and expected him to respond we demonstrated that belief to Jonathan and ourselves. All training, listening, and learning were and are continuous activities done in the meaningful context of daily experiences instead of isolated sessions in a sheltered environment.

Following the premise that Jonathan deserved the same chance to succeed or fail that we might give any of our other children, Jonathan started private nursery school with normally hearing children at the age of three and entered his local neighborhood public school in grade one. That first day was far more traumatic for mother than child. Jonathan repeatedly teaches me that the fears and problems are more mine than his.

He entered grade one with language skills of a four year old, speech skills of a two-to-three year old, and reading skills of a seven year old. By grade two the margin had narrowed considerably, and with the exception of mathematics, he graduated in the upper half of grade three. His math troubles, however, are not necessarily related to his hearing impairment but rather to a weakness that's directly "inherited" from both his parents.

Like most of his friends and children in the neighborhood, Jonathan's week is a busy one. He regularly attends the weekly after-school programs which include crafts and drama projects, goes skating and swimming with his friends, plays floor hockey on the street or in the gym, belongs to the neighborhood Cub Scouts pack, and just recently was on the winning soccer team in our community. He has also attended day camps every summer since the age of four and this past summer spent an additional two weeks in a local tennis camp. Recently, he was one of seventy children from his school who spent four days at an outdoor education centre, 150 miles north of the city.

Three years ago we finally gave in to Jonathan and enrolled him in a Hebrew school. He attends two hours three times a week (twice after school as well as Sunday mornings) and is learning to read, write and speak Hebrew at grade level.

After seven years with Louise Crawford, he continues auditory training in the North York General Hospital program with Warren Estabrooks (see Lessons with Older Children, page 171. The main focus of our early years of training centred on building Jonathan's language skills and little attention was given to the quality of his speech. However, as the linguistic gap of his development narrowed considerably, we began to pay more attention to his speech skills. Consequently, during these last two years, the auditory training sessions have focused equally on listening skills and speech targets, and the results have been staggering. For example, he now includes, quite unconsciously, the "s" sound in his running speech, although initially he didn't hear it, and had no idea how to produce it. He has learned to listen for such specific sounds, and monitors his own speech production to make sure that they are incorporated into his own speech. The reward for Jonathan has been better intelligibility to all those around him and that, in effect, is the motivation that forces him continuously on.

His support system has always remained constant. We do daily work together at home practising some auditory and speech targets, and work together on his homework whenever necessary. His homework load has always been an exceptionally heavy one, because of his extra needs and activities. French, for example, is a new daily subject in grade four. He gets school homework and Hebrew homework, as well as work to be done for the itinerant teacher, who sees him twice a week in school on a one-to-one basis. One of her projects this year will be working on telephone skills (see Telephone Training, page 175). In a few short weeks Jonathan has learned to actively differentiate between a dial tone, busy signal, and the ringing of the telephone. He is able to identify many simple directions and messages over the telephone and as a result has begun to enjoy the use of the telephone that we all take for granted. He can now call and arrange meetings with friends and phone home whenever necessary. His progress is continuous and we now see the telephone as part of his future. Auditory training and his continuous use of his residual hearing have surely formed the foundation for this skill: the telephone allows for no visual clues to rely upon.

Jonathan has always been an aggressively independent child. For the last three or four years he has travelled regularly on his own to visit his grandparents, an hour's flight from home, and has always returned with the addresses of newly made acquaintances. He spends hours at our local Y on his own or with friends, phoning when he is ready to be picked up. And after years of badgering, he finally succeeded in convincing us once again that we had better not put limits on his interests — he now takes weekly piano lessons and will perform in his first recital at Christmas time.

Jonathan's teacher says of him: "Jonathan is an outgoing pupil who enjoys all aspects of the school program. He has made very good academic progress. He reads a variety of materials with great interest and good comprehension and retention. His own stories exhibit an active imagination and creativity. Jonathan has a pleasing personality and gets along well with his peers."

Vanessa

Vanessa is now eleven years old and in grade six at her local public school. She attended the auditory training program at The Hospital for Sick Children until she was nine years old and since has been going to a private tutor once every two weeks. She also receives help at school from an itinerant teacher twice a week. Both teachers have continued an auditory approach in working with Vanessa. For over a year Vanessa has worn two ear level aids instead of body aids. She prefers the ear level aids now and seems to do just as well with them.

In the past five years, Vanessa has virtually overcome her handicap. Her speech and language have developed so well that many people, meeting her for the first time, are quite surprised when they find out she has a profound hearing loss. "But she's not **really** deaf, is she?" they usually ask.

Vanessa's achievement is largely the result of her own motivation and her own efforts in recent years. Between the ages of four to about eight, she really resented having to do auditory training lessons with me. "It isn't fair. Other children don't have to work like this," was a constant complaint. As she grew older, however, she began to realize the real implications of her deafness. She realized that the world is a noisy place and that she was missing out on a lot. She also realized that if she spoke and people didn't understand her, it was because she was not speaking clearly or correctly. By the time she was nine, she was the one who insisted on doing lessons, and became upset if we didn't have time to do one. She began to check the pronunciation of words with me constantly, and so our auditory training took a different approach. A great deal of it was done spontaneously and was initiated by her. After so many years of planning and organizing lessons, and then persuading Vanessa to do them, this was a welcome change.

When Vanessa was about 10, she had an opportunity to meet some deaf children her age who primarily used manual communication and who did not have intelligible speech, and she became quite interested in the whole subject of deafness, particularly why some children learn to talk and others don't. From this point on, she took great pride in her own achievement. She also wanted to know why my husband and I wanted her to learn to speak rather than learn sign language.

We explained to her that there were many reasons that we wanted her to learn to speak. By learning to speak, she could talk freely with anyone — her grandparents, all her aunts, uncles and cousins, her neighbors, and anyone else she happened to encounter in normal everyday life. A person who knows only sign language can communicate only with those few people who know sign language. We explained that we wanted her to live at home with us and go to our neighborhood school, not a special school far away from where we lived. We also explained to her that the door of manual communication is not closed to her. She can always learn sign language at any time in the future if she wishes. Certainly if she had been educated manually from infancy, the opposite would not be possible. If a child's residual hearing is left dormant and listening skills not developed at a very early age, it is unlikely that that child will ever be able to learn to speak. Vanessa understands these things now. "I'm so glad you made me do Miss Crawford's lessons, Mom," she has told me repeatedly.

As a parent, you always have doubts about whether or not you are doing the right or the best things for your child. These doubts are certainly intensified when you have a child with a handicap. My husband and I now feel that we did do the right thing; Vanessa is so normal in every way.

Every morning there is a race between Vanessa and her father to get the newspaper first. She teases, bickers, fools around and fights with her younger brothers in the normal fashion. She is very popular with children in the neighborhood and at school and is frequently invited to sleep overnight or to go to a movie or a birthday party. She is an excellent swimmer, has been on the school swim team and is taking special diving lessons this year. For the past two summers she has gone to a month long camp and enjoyed this experience. She wants to get her ears pierced like the other girls in her class and argues constantly with me about her clothes. She is also learning to use the telephone, much to her delight. The more she uses it, the better she becomes at understanding what the other person is saying.

Vanessa's life is not without problems. She has to be alert at all times in school to follow what the teacher and other students are saying and to know what is going on, and this tires her out a great deal. Also, she is frustrated in many group social situations. She cannot follow all the banter and chatter completely and so often feels left out. But she has close friendships with several girls and these compensate for her frustration. While her speech is good, she still must do speech drill and listening exercises regularly and probably will always have to.

In school, Vanessa has always done well. She is an excellent speller, reads at grade level and has no problems with math. To quote from her grade five report: "It is a pleasure to teach such a fine student." No exceptions are made for her in standard of work expected and kinds of assignments. Recently she received a B on her oral public speaking presentation, an A in her social studies project, and an A+ in her science project. Much of her success in school is due to the attitudes, the work habits, and the ability to attend and concentrate which she learned in her early years of auditory training. Teachers have always commented on how carefully she pays attention and on her excellent work habits. Next year she'll be going to a senior public school where she'll have four or five different subject teachers each day. She is a little anxious but basically looking forward to this new challenge.

The other day she was reading a newspaper article about 1981 being International Year of the Disabled. She looked up, her eyes twinkling, and asked, "Mom, am I disabled?" And then she laughed.

Richard

*Richard is now ten years old. He wears two
ear level hearing aids. He is in grade five
in his local public school. He went to the
Hospital for Sick Children for auditory
training until he was almost nine years old.
He then did auditory and speech work with a
private tutor for a year. Now he is in an
auditory training program at the North York
General Hospital. He is an avid hockey
player, takes piano and trumpet lessons and is
a happy, outgoing boy.*

Richard's audiogram has not changed in five-and-a-half
years, since I first wrote about him, but many friends and
relatives insist that his hearing is "improving all the time."
Even though they mean a different kind of improvement,
nevertheless, they are right: for all practical purposes his
hearing is improving. He can hear sounds that a few years
ago he didn't know existed: the ticking of a clock, the
dripping water tap, and the crackling of burning wood. Now,
like many hearing people, he demands quiet when he is
concentrating — noises distract him. All this is almost hard
to believe when I think back to his first years in auditory
training — one could practically shoot a cannon behind his
back and he wouldn't turn around.

When Richard was about to start grade school, his
language was still quite limited and his listening habits not
yet at their best. We knew that in order for him to succeed in
a regular classroom he would need an accepting attitude in
his teachers. This could be accomplished with the help of an
understanding and supportive principal. We found all of
this in our local public school.

As his language matures and his listening skills
improve, he needs less and less extra help to cope with his
schoolwork. It is exhilarating to see his independence grow
from year to year. In the previous grades, despite the help he

was getting at school, there was always some schoolwork to be done at home. This year, with the support of his classroom teacher and the itinerant teacher who comes twice a week, he is able to handle his grade five work virtually without my help, French being the only exception.

Once a week we go to a speech and auditory training teacher. In the two years since we started to work directly on the quality of his speech it has improved dramatically. In our daily lessons we work on his speech as well as increasing his vocabulary and expanding his general knowledge.

A year ago we started Richard on trumpet lessons, hoping that it would lead to a better perception of sound and aid his speech through improved breathing. This year he started taking piano lessons. The fact that his brother and sister have been taking piano lessons perhaps made him go along with our suggestion that he take them, too. So far his rapid progress and musical talent have surprised us.

Like many boys his age he has a passion for hockey. He has been playing for the local house league for three years. The last two years he has been chosen for the Select Team.

It took many years of hard work to get where he is now, the most difficult part being that we had to persevere with auditory training throughout prolonged periods of illness and seemingly endless periods of "learning plateaus", but the results have brought us all an extraordinary sense of fulfilment. Up till now it has been our responsibility to give him every opportunity to develop to the full his potential for growth in every aspect of his personality. We chose what we thought was the best way for him and for the rest of our family. We still think so. From a child who was rebellious, withdrawn and uncommunicative, he has developed into a mature, self-reliant and happy individual, who feels comfortable in the hearing world and is able to cope effectively with whatever problems may arise due to his handicap. He will still need our support in the years to come, but it is our hope and belief that by the time he reaches adulthood he will be a well-rounded and independent individual. And that, I think, is the greatest gift parents can give their child.

The principal of Richard's school wrote of him: "Richard has made exceptional progress in the five years he has attended this school. Teachers who worked with him in his first year and then again three or four years later have found a great improvement in his speech and in his awareness of sound. He is currently achieving at a grade five level in all subjects.

"He is a very popular boy and is one of the first boys picked when teams are being set up. He has good study habits and works well independently.

"Although the teachers he has had are exceptionally capable professionals, they feel that an important factor in Richard's development is the support of his family along with the regular and consistent support provided by the itinerant teacher who works with him twice a week."

Peter

Peter is eight years old now and in grade three at his local public school. He has always been integrated with his hearing peers. Peter is in Cubs, goes to Sunday school, takes swimming and skating lessons, took art lessons and gymnastics, goes camping, and participates in baseball and soccer. His achievement records indicate that he has been doing as well as his peers in all activities. Peter receives itinerant help at school, and since he graduated from the auditory training program at the Hospital for Sick Children, he has been going to the auditory program at North York General Hospital once a week.

During Peter's first years in school, I would go into his classroom and take pictures of his teachers and the other children to help him learn their names. I used to tape the songs used in school and sing them with Peter at home. I visited Peter's classroom as often as possible to find out what was being taught and noted such things as how the teacher greeted the children, what material was taught first thing in the morning, which games were played, and what kinds of materials were displayed on the walls.

All this has changed now. Peter's teacher feels that he does not need any help with his school work. His teachers have always expressed surprise at his general knowledge. This is because I try to expose him to as many aspects of our world as I can. Sometimes my eagerness results in embarrassment; e.g., last week, on our visit to the Art Gallery, I was explaining to Peter the impressionists' use of colors, and he announced, "I am not blind, I can see!" Similarly, when at an early age we went to his first symphony concert, he loudly protested, "You make too much noise!"

When I read newspapers or magazines, I clip pictures or news stories which might interest Peter. Even some advertisements are enriching, such as the advertisement of diamonds which led to a wide discussion from mining to the colonization of Africa. Since his curiosity surpasses my knowledge, I direct him to the appropriate book and sometimes I have to explain what is written in the encyclopedia. On a trip, I buy maps of the city, history books, postcards, and I collect things like napkins and ticket stubs which I paste in his diary hoping for a story, but I usually get just a sentence or two. Peter loves reading, and likes to dictate stories to me, but he hates writing.

Because Peter learned to read earlier than his hearing peers, Peter made a good impression on his teachers and principal; but most importantly, he was able to acquire different grammatical structures and, as mentioned in his last report card, a "vast oral vocabulary". I read a great deal to him till we started making agreements such as "I read one page and you read the other." We read candy wrappers, gum wrappers, gas station signs, store signs, and many other things, as well as books. Although I believe that today Peter's reading speed is greater than mine, I still feel that I should read poetry to him for pitch and intonation. From his conversations, I am certain that I am no longer the main source of Peter's language or information.

However, every week there are new words and expressions to be taught. Some of our current words and expressions are "excruciating", "snicker", "hearth", "go fly a kite", and "itchy fingers." By the end of a week, he has to be able to define each word or expression and use each in a few sentences.

Our daily (and I do not want to imply that lessons are not missed!) formal auditory training exercises are done from behind him, and according to his listening ability, I move further and further back. He has to repeat the sounds a(r), ee, oo, sh, and s from increasing distances. Similarly he has to repeat children's spondee words such as sidewalk, birthday, cupcake, airplane, and headlight. Then, he has to answer questions from "What's your name?" to "What's your favorite kind of ice cream?" When we started this exercise we used to work on the same questions for months. I also read numbers from behind, such as 1,587 or 1,234 or 6,009, and he has to write them down. We play educational games designed to develop and improve math, language and thinking skills.

Peter enjoys music and singing. When his auditory training teacher plays his guitar while singing nursery rhymes or popular children's songs behind Peter, Peter is unable to identify them, but we are continuing to work in this area. Peter is also learning to use the telephone, to discriminate messages from a tape recorder, and to listen to the news.

Although Peter's speech is good, I always keep a list of the words that he mispronounces. Most of these words are the ones that he has picked up on his own. We practice a few of them every week, and when he can say them correctly he makes up a sentence for each one. I keep the list for future review.

At the age of four, Peter rebelled against his lessons. Although I varied the lessons in order to have a pleasant activity followed by a hard one, or tried to invent ways to make a hard activity pleasant, he did not want to do certain things. I tried positive reinforcement, negative reinforcement, reasoning, and threats. None of them was effective for all activities. Lately, very firmly and with all my authority, I state, "You have told me before that you don't like writing stories and I have explained to you why you have to do it. Co-operate, because I don't want to stay here all night."

Sometimes unpleasantness occurs when Peter is with other children in settings that lack adult supervision. At those times, he rarely plays quiet games or board games but he prefers to run and chase the other children, play with guns or have play fights. Although this problem could be attributed to many factors, I feel that his personality in combination with his hearing impairment and people's reactions to it are the main reasons for a tense atmosphere. Therefore, at this point of his development, I feel that socialization is the priority. As a result, when a child calls on Peter, I am willing to stop a lesson or miss it altogether so they can play.

Looking back, so many things have changed for the best. The guilt for my child's hearing impairment has vanished, and the time spent on structured teaching is approximately one-tenth of what it was in the beginning. Peter's teacher told us last year that Peter was "a little miracle" because, despite his hearing impairment, he was doing better than most of the children in his class. We are very proud of Peter, and watching him grow is a joy and a challenge. We are amused by his good sense of humor and have satisfying conversations with him.

I am especially delighted that in spite of our close relationship and the large amounts of time I have spent with him, he is by no means my follower. For instance, a few days ago when I was explaining the causes, results and implications of a coma and expressing my opinion on the issue of euthanasia, Peter adopted the radically different opinion and stated very firmly that, "Doctors should never give up on people."

Matthew

*Matthew is now twelve years old and is in grade
seven at the local Roman Catholic school where
he is doing well. He has a ten-year-old brother,
Timothy. His mother is not presently employed
outside the home but worked part-time for
four years (when he was seven to eleven years
of age). Matthew tests as being "severely deaf",
but after several years of auditory training,
he responds as a hard of hearing child when
he is wearing his aids. He wears two
body aids outside the classroom, and has
used an FM unit at school for the past
two-and-a-half years.*

In December, 1979, when Matthew was eleven, we moved
from Toronto to Sarnia. Had he not had the advantage early
in his life of excellent auditory training and language
development programs, we would not have felt free to move
to a smaller centre. We will always be grateful to Matthew's
teachers and to the many parents who supported us.

At first Matthew did not feel comfortable in his new
school, but by March his teacher reported, "He appears to
have adjusted to his new environment very nicely. He seems
quite content and gets along well with his classmates.
Matthew is mentally alert and grasps information quickly."

He was having some difficulty with math and spelling
but was making "excellent progress" in music. Math was
always fairly difficult for him, and though he was not failing
this subject, we felt he needed extra help. For a year and a
half, in grades five and six, we took him to a private tutor.
His math has improved but he continues to need regular
assistance from us.

His classmates in Sarnia had had a great deal more
instruction in French than he had been exposed to and
consequently this is his poorest subject. This year Matthew

is getting private tutorial help from his French teacher and is slowly improving. His grade seven home-room teacher sees him as "an extremely capable student", but feels he must put forth more effort in order to attain his potential.

For some time around the ages of nine to ten years, Matthew expressed anger and resentment about his hearing impairment and the extra work he had to do. He now seems to have accepted his handicap and no longer speaks of it in such negative terms. On one occasion I remarked that if he and I had not worked very hard he would not be able to hear or speak as well as he does. His immediate response was, "If you had not worked hard with me, I would have been very mad at you later on." Recently, his French teacher told him that he would learn to speak French by asking questions just as he had learned English. He replied, "My Mom taught me English."

At present Matthew has no outside help except for French. For a variety of reasons (sore ears due to badly fitting earmoulds, adjustments to the move, etc.), in the last several months we did not pay as much attention to auditory training as we should have. Consequently, he is not presently listening as well as he used to, and we have begun once again to concentrate on his auditory skills. It is most important to remember that these skills need constant attention.

Matthew is a well-rounded young boy. He used to play hockey and was a Beaver and a Cub. He plays squash, racquet ball, tennis, golf, and likes to swim. Last summer he won a golf trophy and was extremely proud of his achievement.

For the last three years he has taken recorder lessons and will soon play in a Christmas concert. Though not a great musician, he entertains us with his limited repertoire. We, his parents, prefer this to the rock and roll music he is addicted to. We have to make sure his record player and radio are turned off when he is doing his homework. He also plays the drums in his school band.

162

Matthew is an avid reader, and particularly enjoys mysteries and space stories. He also likes comics and *Mad Magazine*.

An update on Matthew would be incomplete without reference to his great propensity to argue. He questions everything and does an admirable job of attempting to talk us out of having him do something he prefers to avoid. (Oh, when I think of the years I spent dreaming and hoping he might some day talk in sentences!!) However, we continue to expect him to perform certain chores and to behave in a socially acceptable manner.

His progress still delights us, and we are extremely proud of the way our son participates and belongs in the world around him. He is truly a normal person who just happens to have a hearing impairment.

John

John is ten years old and in grade five at his local public school. He recently experimented with an ear level aid but he himself felt he could not hear as well. Currently, John is using a body aid with only his right ear. For classroom use, he has an FM unit and is responsible for informing the itinerant teacher when it is out of order. An itinerant teacher monitors his performance weekly and spends time on enrichment activities. His speech skills are good. John's pediatrician also monitors his physical and psychosocial development.

John has established a good relationship with a variety of people. His rapport with teachers is good; they have frequently commented on his sense of humor and inquiring nature. His teachers have indicated that John has much potential for academic success and has not displayed any major problems coping with curriculum demands including French.

John graduated from the Auditory Training Program at The Hospital for Sick Children when he was eight years old. He expressed concern about this separation. One can appreciate the impact that a special teacher has on these children when they are mature enough to realize how much of their learning depends on a commitment to auditory training. One cannot put a price on the value of such a relationship.

While visiting relatives, John has questioned his grandfather about the family tree. His cousins share their friends and time. He enjoys their friendship and is not hesitant to speak his mind or have a healthy heated discussion. I did observe, however, that while in the pool he misses a lot of cues while playing a water sport. This creates some frustration. Sometimes he misses normal interaction and finds it distressing when suddenly one of his cousins goes off with another friend. He hasn't been able to mobilize his own feelings adequately to prepare for a disappointment.

John is much like his peers. He enjoys special relationships with children his own age. His school chums come from a variety of cultural backgrounds and this has a tremendous influence on his learning and language development. He is sociable and sensitive to the differences in these children and most of his hearing peers are quite perceptive regarding his handicap. He has had a few incidents at school and summer camp which have frustrated him but he was able to discuss these and thus cope better; e.g., he stated that he always gets chosen last when children are selecting teams for outdoor activities.

He has developed a sense of competitiveness and likes to do well at school. He also enjoys Boy Brigade at which time he interacts with children in a group and in a one-to-one relationship. With his friends, he plays games, trades books or works on projects. His favorite games include *Monopoly*, *Strategies*, and *Battleship*. His other interests are swimming, cycling, and collecting stamps, coins, and rocks.

John's telephone skills have improved so that he can independently comprehend most of the conversation. He recently was able to take a friend's number and discriminate that she had laryngitis, which he described as a weak voice. We encourage him to use the phone, a skill which will be important for independent living. At this time he does show a degree of impatience to get the conversation over with. He often indicates that he has a hearing problem and people respond appropriately.

Over the years we have encouraged John to develop a positive self-image. He displays trust by sharing time and experiences. He expresses himself openly on many issues; i.e., he is not afraid to disagree. He shows initiative in that he starts projects eagerly and demonstrates original thoughts; e.g., in grade four he created a game about volcanoes and adapted it to a *Monopoly* game. His sense of industry is manifest in tasks he has completed, and in his willingness to work with others. His use of time is quite effective.

John's interaction with others is spontaneous and he appears confident about the decisions he makes. When he was nine he was confident enough to travel on the subway to downtown Toronto, buy his lunch, and shop for new pants. On arriving at summer camp and after looking the camp over, John let us know that his decision was to stay no longer than one week. He is sensitive and can express himself in a compassionate way.

John derives hours of pleasure from reading. Looking to the future, this will provide a release from some of the frustrations which the hearing impaired inevitably experience.

At this time John's relationship with his parents is special. He communicates new ideas, experiences and thoughts about himself. He is quite mature for a ten year old and has perhaps discussed issues many ten year olds would not be aware of. There are times when he has expressed great concern about being an only child. There are times when we have had doubts about his self-esteem when he comes home and tells us he has no friends or that he gets chosen last, but in comparing the positive with the negative and in looking at his accomplishments we have concluded that John has a healthy self-image.

Auditory training — A teacher's update

by Louise Crawford

Most of the children I work with, even those with profound hearing losses, are now wearing an ear level aid in each ear. I sit beside the child and speak to him in a normal tone of voice. However, I would suggest, if for some reason the child is only able to wear one ear level hearing aid, that the teacher sit on the aided side of the child in order to be closer to his or her microphone. Likewise, if the child is known to have significantly more hearing in one ear than the other, it makes sense for the teacher to sit beside the better ear.

During the past few years, I have had the opportunity of seeing a number of children in the six-to-twelve-month age group on a weekly basis. These children all have profound hearing losses. In addition to counselling the parents to sing and talk close to their child, I have also instructed them to play with the toys described in Sample lesson A (see page 77). We present one toy at a time and talk about it, repeating the appropriate sound as we play. By twelve months of age, the children have shown signs of associating some of the sounds with the appropriate objects and in some cases have attempted to say the sounds themselves.

I think it is important that parents have regular and frequent meetings with either a teacher or an audiologist during the first few months after their child has been fitted with hearing aids. This is particularly necessary in the case of infants. Most parents have had no previous experience with hearing aids. They do not always recognize the various problems that can beset an aid, may not know when it is time to get new earmoulds, and often need help in fitting the aids comfortably and securely to their child.

If parents are not supported during this period, it is quite likely that their child will not make a good adjustment to his aids or that defects will go undetected for a long period of time.

Remember that a child must wear his hearing aids all his waking hours and they must be kept in excellent working order if he is going to learn to listen.

Lessons with older children

by Warren Estabrooks

Since the six children described in this edition of *Learning to Listen* have had a number of years of auditory training, the following is a sample lesson plan which I follow when teaching "older" children.

1. The five-sound test. This is done to make sure the aids are working properly. I stand behind or next to the child and say the following sounds: a(r) as in father; oo as in pool; ee as in feet; sh, and s as in supper. If the child repeats these correctly, his hearing aid is functioning adequately and he is probably hearing across the frequencies. Inconsistent performance on this test could indicate impacted wax or fluid in the middle ear.

2. Discussion. We discuss a topic of particular interest to the child, such as a family or school event. This puts the child at ease.

3. Auditory questions. I usually ask a series of ten questions, two of which will be new and may contribute to development of vocabulary or new linguistic structures.

4. Speech skills. I generally follow the classic works of Dr. Daniel Ling, Doreen Pollack, the Ewings, G. Sybley Haycock, plus my own skills which one can learn only experientially. At three different times during the lesson, I work on the targets which have been determined from phonetic and phonologic assessment. These include the subskills for targets, plus reviewing the skills which the children have practised at home during the week with their parents. The aim here is also to help the parents acquire some of the teaching strategies. The limited time we may devote to speech skills in the clinic is simply not

171

enough to develop the transfer we desire into spoken English. I also work on words, phrases and sentences, incorporating appropriate targets. We play speech games such as *Password* to encourage transfer.

5. Crossword puzzle by audition. This activity varies depending on which skills I need to reinforce. Sometimes the crossword is based on words which all begin with "ch." This implies that the child may have been working with this target for some time and I want to reinforce the target in a meaningful and enjoyable way. Other puzzles may involve particular language principles such as antonyms or synonyms. I find it is also a good method for testing and enriching vocabulary. I ask the child to listen to the clue and write the corresponding answer in the appropriate space.

6. Writing numerals by audition. I ask the student to write down ten numerals. The child competes with himself. I have found my students listening intently for minute differences in difficult numerals such as 6332 and 8203.

7. Poetry. The children memorize poetry. The aims here are to develop auditory and visual memory, to practise speech skills, to discuss poetic devices and poetic license, and to enrich vocabulary. Poems are chosen for interest but also to illustrate rhythm and rate.

8. Auditory story. Often I write the stories about my own students, and then present a series of questions to test the child's comprehension. I read the story **once** behind the child, and then pose the questions. Often a clue to some missed piece of information is inherent in the questions. If a child misses an answer I will read the story again. Self-competition is used as an incentive. When the student has acquired all the answers, the child reads the story into the tape recorder. This provides another opportunity to enrich specific speech skills. We play the tape back and evaluate the presentation together.

9. Vocabulary. Each week the child is responsible for learning approximately eight to ten new words, idioms, or expressions. The student learns the definitions and sentences to demonstrate the appropriate meaning. The vocabulary is derived from a variety of sources, and I discuss these sources with the parents, who often have an excellent understanding of the specific vocabulary needs. I keep a record of learned vocabulary and retest words when necessary.

10. Written stories. Many students write a story each week which we correct together and which the child rewrites for the following week. This affords me the opportunity to observe grammatical errors and thus I am able to plan grammar lessons for following weeks.

11. Picture descriptions. I present an interesting picture which the child then uses as a source for descriptive, narrative, or imaginative stories. This encourages oral expression, application of grammar rules, usage of new vocabulary, and provides an opportunity to evaluate speech and expressive linguistic structures.

12. Riddles and jokes. I try to provide an opportunity to share an understanding of puns, riddles, and jokes which many other children may learn by overhearing others.

13. Games. These vary from the use of sequence stories, to matching games, grammar and speech games, and reinforcement activities for concepts and vocabulary.

14. Newspaper articles. The student prepares a short newspaper article to read and then asks me a series of questions to test my comprehension. I can say that often my comprehension is far below that of my students because I find myself concentrating so hard on articulation that I forget to really listen! These students are **my** teachers.

15. Music. I incorporate music into each lesson. I like to play the guitar for my children and have them listen to songs, nursery rhymes, and poems set to music. Music is part of all cultures and the joy of listening to a hearing impaired child singing never ceases to give me a thrill.

This is a basic lesson plan. Of course, any lesson varies according to goals. In essence, we all share the teaching roles. The parents of these students are indeed **my** teachers, and together we work to help our children realize their potential in an auditory verbal environment.

Using the telephone

by Dorothy R. Boothroyd

Using the telephone is a means of communication which is taken for granted by a hearing person. For the profoundly hearing impaired individual, however, it is a skill which must be learned. While three of the children in this book had already acquired this skill, Jonathan at the age of nine had not and was most anxious to do so. The following is a description of some techniques which I used in training him to use the telephone.

At home Jonathan uses an Impaired Hearing Handset which was bought from Bell Canada. Away from home he has a portable telephone amplifier which was purchased at Radio Shack for $18.98. Although the telephones we use have a magnetic field, Jonathan chose to use the microphone (M) rather than the telephone (T) setting of the ear level hearing aid on his better ear.

At the beginning of this project Jonathan was given a notebook to record each step so that intensive and consistent training could occur at home and at school. A brief introduction to the purposes and importance of the telephone was followed by learning the basic signals. After discussing all-important telephone etiquette, we proceeded to a very simple conversation which Jonathan initiated and controlled. He had to get information by asking questions to which the response could only be "yes yes" (2 syllables), "no" (1 syllable), or "please repeat" (3 syllables). This code was typed on cards and distributed to family and friends who were called for practice. We then worked on listening to the time, the day, and the month. Jonathan learned to comprehend messages of increasing difficulty: "Please come at 4 o'clock; come on Wednesday; come on Wednesday at 4 o'clock; come on Wednesday, November 7 at 4 o'clock."

Identifying places and people's names was next: "This is Mrs. Boothroyd calling. Can you come over to my house on Monday at 3 o'clock?" It is only occasionally possible for Jonathan to identify a speaker by voice alone over the telephone.

After the above activities were mastered, we proceeded to work on familiar questions: "When is your birthday? Where do you live?" We then began more unstructured conversations. These are still difficult for Jonathan and at this point it is impossible to predict the full extent to which he will be able to use the telephone.

If problems of comprehension occur during any of the tasks which have been described, Jonathan employs specifically taught strategies to ascertain the necessary information. If two repetitions of numbers are unsuccessful, he may ask the other person to count or he himself may ask, "Did you say one?", "Did you say two?", etc. The same procedure of asking questions is used for the days and months. In other situations he will ask for the key word. If this too is incomprehensible, he will ask the person to spell the word either with letters or with code words which have been chosen by Jonathan as easy to discriminate. The latter are typed on cards for the use of family and friends. If, for example, Jonathan were having difficulty understanding the key word "movie", the other person could spell it in code words as follows: mommy-open-Victoria-India-elephant.

Most recently we have worked on emergency telephone calls. Jonathan had to memorize the emergency numbers and the following message which is also on a card near his telephone: "Hello. This is an emergency. My name is Jonathan _____ . I am deaf. There is a fire in my house. Please send help to 123 Main Street. I said 1-2-3 Main Street."

Learning to use the telephone is a new listening experience which requires a structured approach and continuous practice. Listening, speech and language are integral parts of this training and must be considered at all times. Using the telephone has become a vital part of our everyday life. Hearing impaired children should be given the opportunity to acquire this skill and use it to their optimum potential.

Parents, be aware!

by Dorothy Scott

The terms "Acoupedic", "Auditory/Oral", "Aural/Oral", "Auditory Approach", "Auditory Method", "Auditory Option", "Auditory Training" and "Auditory-Verbal Communication" are the different terms that describe the following approach: the training being given to the child is directed towards training the defective sense, hearing. Like the children in this book, the child is trained to use and rely on residual hearing. The child is expected to process the sound to develop speech and language in the same way that normal children learn to talk. It is essential to deliver such training on an individual basis.

The terms "Auditory/Oral", "Oral", "Aural/Oral", and "Pure Oral" describe a *combined* visual and auditory training approach used to help the child develop speech and language. The child is trained to watch the faces of speakers in order to understand (through lipreading). Adults address the child using normal speech and expect a verbal response. This type of combination approach can lay more or less stress on vision and hearing.

The terms "Hearing Training", "Auditory Component", or more popularly, "Total Communication", describe a training where some auditory stimulation is being given along with much visual input, including some form of manual language (finger spelling, sign language). Many schools, especially residential, use such methods, giving very little attention to the auditory potential of hearing impaired childen.

Parents must make sure that their child is getting the kind of training they want him to have.

Hearing aids today

Since *Learning to Listen* was published, hearing aids have become much more sophisticated. Ear level aids have become more powerful and often have better frequency response, so more children may now be fitted with them.

Today, almost all hearing impaired childen are fitted binaurally, i.e., with two hearing aids, one for each ear. Once aids have been prescribed and fitted, put the aids on the child and make sure he wears them as much as possible as soon as possible. The earlier a child wears his aids, be they body aids or ear level aids, the less problem he has adapting and the chances of optimum use of residual hearing are better.

The main advantage of ear level aids is that they enable the wearer to localize the source of sound more easily. Because the microphones are placed on each ear, the localizing function of normally hearing ears is duplicated in the closest audiological way possible.

Furthermore, ear level aids now have such sophisticated controls that they can be set to emphasize the high rather than the low frequencies and thus give the child more of the clues on which the intelligibility of speech depends.

Parents have reported that very young infants often pull their aids out. When this becomes a problem, a special hypoallergenic tape can be used to tape the aids to the mastoid bone.

The problem of getting a properly fitting earmould may be the same whether the child wears body aids or ear level aids.

Many audiologists still prefer to fit a very young infant with body aids. Because a young child spends much of his time either lying down, or actively bouncing about, they feel that body aids serve a better function as the first set of hearing aids. Audiologist and teacher can, therefore, decide which is the best fitting for each particular child.

Today, many hearing impaired childen who are integrated in regular classrooms wear an FM system at school. In such a system, the teacher wears a microphone transmitter. The pupil wears a large body aid which contains two separate hearing aid units, one for each ear. The teacher's voice can come directly into the child's aids without the distortion caused by intervening noise. At the same time, the aids can pick up nearby sound just as a regular aid does. When the teacher's transmitter is turned off, the child's system acts just like a regular aid so that there is no need to "undress" for recess or noon hour.

These systems run on batteries which must be recharged daily. This can be done by the parent or the pupil himself. As with ordinary hearing aids, the FM system should be regularly checked to make sure microphone-transmitter and receiver are functioning properly.

Recently a personalized FM System has been developed. With this, the teacher wears a microphone-transmitter much as before, but the pupil wears a smaller receiver box attached to a belt, with a "boot" connected directly into his own hearing aids. The hearing aids remain on the regular microphone setting but function as an FM unit all the time the teacher's microphone is in action. Should the personal aids and the FM unit be made by different manufacturers, the child wears a "loop" around his neck. The loop creates a magnetic field which enables the child's own hearing aids to pick up the sound when set at "telephone". Ideally, such an aid should have an MT setting so that other voices may be picked up too. The advantage of such a system is its portability. Another advantage is that the child remains on one consistent sound system and need not change into different hearing aids before and after school. Some teenagers accept this system well and may prefer it for the obvious cosmetic reasons; others dislike it, complaining of distortion and lack of power. Unlike the regular FM system, this system is removed for recess, lunch, gym, etc., and requires some personal tending to by the child.

Because of the smaller size and cost, some schools and classes have started using this personalized FM System with preschoolers. There are many switches to turn on and off and consequently many things that can go wrong. The more sections you add to an auditory system, the less amplification and frequency response you get. It is probably better to wait a few years until things get sorted out before trying this kind of aid with very young children who haven't yet a clear idea of what sound should be like for them and who are not mature enough to look after their own amplification system by themselves.

Fitting a hearing aid is becoming a more and more specialized business. New techniques for increasing the efficiency of earmoulds are being developed all the time. New ways of using aids to increase frequency response are also being developed; such as the CROS fitting for those with unequal losses in the two ears or the dichotic fitting in which two aids with different frequency responses are used.

More than ever **it is essential that your child's aids be fitted by a properly qualified audiologist, one who has had experience in fitting very young children and who is willing and interested in following the auditory progress of the child on a regular basis.** Educational audiology implies the active participation of the audiologist, teachers, and parents as a team.

Part VI

Services available

Bibliography

Glossary

Services available to parents

1. **The Canadian Hearing Society**
   60 Bedford Rd.,
   Toronto, M5R 2K2
   Telephone: (416) 964–9595.

The Society provides audiological services and an information service. In the Audiology department, university trained Audiologists perform hearing evaluations and make hearing aid selections. Their services are free. Enquire about the Hearing Aid Program which allows for the purchase of hearing aids through your local Parents' Association. The Society may be contacted for the name of your local parents' association.

The Information Services provide information concerning resources and make available books, pamphlets and catalogues of educational materials. There is a library, open to the public, with a wide range of books on the subject.

Another service sponsored by the Canadian Hearing Society is:

2. **Parent Sharing Group**

Just as its name implies, this is a group of parents of hearing impaired children who have volunteered to meet and talk with parents of newly diagnosed hearing impaired children. The group is made up entirely of parents who have suffered the same fears that you may be suffering and have, believe it or not, survived and discovered that life can go on happily. The next time you feel like pulling your hair out, remember that another parent is available to talk to you. She will understand how you feel. To be put in touch with a member of Parent Sharing, write or telephone the Canadian Hearing Society.

3. **The Hospital for Sick Children,**
   555 University Avenue, Toronto.

The Ear, Nose and Throat Clinic of the Hospital provides an excellent

Assessment Program for hearing impaired children. Under the medical direction of an Otolaryngologist-in-Chief, a team assesses the "total" child. Social and family information is obtained by a social worker to provide a background against which future plans can be worked out. Audiological testing determines the degree and type of hearing loss and the child is subsequently fitted with a hearing aid. The assessment also includes a complete medical examination and E.C.G., polytome x-rays, eye examination, cortical audiometry and any other consultation felt necessary (such as speech, neurological or psychiatric). An educational therapist may discuss available educational resources. The findings are presented to the parents at a final conference with a medical doctor and the social worker. Follow-up audiological services are available at specified intervals and the social worker is available for on-going parental counselling. Accommodation can be found for families coming from outside the Metropolitan Toronto area by a parent personnel worker at the hospital. Write to the E. N. T. Clinic at the Hospital for further details of this program.

4. **The Alexander Graham Bell Association for the Deaf Inc.,**
   3417 Volta Place, N.W., Washington, D.C. 20007.

The regular $15.00 annual membership fee in this organization entitles you to receive The Volta Review, a monthly journal (published every month except June, July and August) which contains articles by both professionals and parents on the education of hearing impaired children. Books on deafness may be purchased through, or borrowed from, the Association and book lists of recent publications are sent out to members each year. Reprints of articles which have appeared in the Volta Review may also be purchased and lists of these are sent out regularly.

The Alexander Graham Bell Association regularly arranges regional conferences on educational topics of interest to parents of hearing impaired children. These are advertised well in advance in The Volta Review.

5. **Voice for Hearing Impaired Children,**
   P.O. Box 152, Station 'S', Toronto M5M 4L7.
   Telephone: (416) 488-6423

This organization offers you:
a) Emotional support and information gleaned from communicating with other parents.
b) Monthly meetings with local, national and international authorities, speaking on topics pertinent to your child's future, e.g.

education, career development, emotional and social development, integration, audiology, research development, medical breakthroughs, and so on.

c) Two workshops are held each year to deal with the more personal problems of coping with your child at home, such as lessons in the home, language growth in the home, coping with integration, family adjustment to the diagnosis, and so on.

d) Large one- or two-day conferences are occasionally hosted where a number of renowned experts are brought together for your benefit.

e) A comprehensive library of books, pamphlets, cassette recordings and other documentation is available during meetings to help keep members informed of research, technical advances and new methods of hearing and speech development.

f) Hearing aids can be purchased at a reduced rate (with an audiologist's recommendation).

This organization endeavors to see that your children get their fare share of the government attention and purse; that your children's educational opportunities and facilities, be they in special education or integrated settings, maintain a high level consistent with that required for success; that the auditory oral approach as an educational method and as a way of life, continues to be available for all who want it; that early identification, education and amplification become a reality for hearing impaired children.

Voice for Hearing Impaired Children supports the premise that all hearing impaired children should have the opportunity if their parents so choose:

a) to develop their listening skills to their maximum potential;
b) to develop their language skills at the earliest possible age;
c) to develop their oral skills in conjunction with their language growth to attain the highest possible educational level;
d) to integrate into the mainstream of education at the pre-school level if possible, or as soon after as is practical considering the individual child's level of progress;
e) to live and grow up with his family within his own community and in the hearing world.

Membership is open to parents and educators of hearing impaired children and to all other interested persons. Members come from all over Ontario with a large number residing in or near Metropolitan Toronto.

To join, write to P.O. Box 152, Station 'S', Toronto M5M 4L7.

Bibliography

The following are books which we have found to be particularly helpful:

ALPINER et al.   *Talk to Me* (2 manuals)
                                                Williams & Wilkins, 1977
A home study program of language development for the preschool child with hearing impairment.

BITTER, Grant B., Ed.   *Parents in Action*
                                                    A.G. Bell, 1978
"A handbook of experiences with their hearing impaired children", but more than that, there are suggestions for working with childen and for books to read. The Crofts, one of the contributing families, started in the program at the Hospital for Sick Children.

BLOOM, Freddy   *Our Deaf Children*
                                                    Heinemann, 1963
Written by the mother of a severely deaf child. It gives advice and tells of her experiences in a clear down-to-earth style. Probably the most useful book available for parents of hearing impaired children.

CASTLE, Diane L.   *Telephone Training for the Deaf*
                                    N.T.I.D. — Rochester Institute
                                                of Technology, 1980
Dr. Castle is a pioneer in the field of telephone training for the deaf and has prepared this detailed course of study on the subject.

CODY, Dr.   *Your Child's Ear, Nose & Throat.*
                                            A Parent's Medical Guide
                                                    MacMillan, 1974
A very useful book for parents of any child, describing the commonest medical problems in the speech area.

COURTMAN-DAVIES, Mary   *Your Deaf Child's Speech and Language*
                                                Bodley Head, 1979
This English book is full of wonderful ideas for parents working with a hearing impaired child. Every parent — and teacher — should have a copy.

CRAIG et al.   *Your Child's Hearing Aid*
                                                    Dormac, 1976
Information about the care and use of the child's aid, written for parents.

EWING, Sir Alexander and Lady (Ethel) *Hearing Impaired Children under Five*
University of Manchester Press, 1971
A guide for parents and teachers which emphasizes the role of parents in the education of young hearing impaired children.

LABINOWICZ, Ed. *The Piaget Primer: Thinking, Learning, Teaching*
Addison-Wesley, 1980
This book shows, with delightful illustration, the different steps young children go through as they solve problems. You should get it just to keep you from worrying when your baby seems to see life from a different perspective than you do. Good ideas for stimulating work, too.

LING, Agnes & Daniel *Communication Development in the first three years of life*
McGill School of Communication Disorders, 1974
A research paper describing the interaction of parent and child in the normal acquisition of speech and language.

LING, Daniel *Speech and the Hearing Impaired Child*
A.G. Bell, 1976
This is definitely a book for professionals, but, once speech work is started with your child, you must make sure that the teacher is familiar with this approach.

LING, Daniel and Agnes *Aural Habilitation — The Foundations of Verbal Learning in Hearing Impaired Children*
A.G. Bell, 1978
How to work with the child to develop effective speech communication skills.

McCONNELL, FREEMAN & WARD, Paul *Deafness in Childhood*
Vanderbilt University Press, 1971
Information on the problem, giving types of training available.

MILLER, ROHMAN & THOMPSON *Your Child's Hearing and Speech A Guide for Parents*
Charles Thomas, 1974 (paperback)
Describes simply about hearing loss and how it is measured. There is a useful section on the types of aids available. They also give a clear outline on normal and abnormal speech and language development and problems of articulation.

NORTHCOTT, Winifred H. Ed. *The Hearing Impaired Child in a Regular Classroom*
A.G. Bell, 1973
Curriculum Guide: Hearing Impaired Children, Birth to three years and their Parents
A.G. Bell, 1972

Both books give a great number of suggestions for work with children, using an auditory approach, as well as helpful advice on planning future educational placement.

NORTHCOTT, Winifred *I Heard That*
A.G. Bell, 1978

A developmental sequence of listening activities of the young child. Norms are given for the age at which skills are acquired.

POLLACK, Doreen *Educational Audiology for the Limited Hearing Infant*
Charles Thomas, 1970

The principles and techniques of "Acoupedics", an auditory training method from which the procedures described in this book are derived. Mrs. Pollack has been training children aurally for some years and has had excellent results.

SCOTT, Dorothy *Keep On Learning to Listen*
Join In Learning to Listen
VOICE, 1979

These books were produced for a VOICE Conference "Learning to Listen: The First Option". The first book gives suggestions for parents who want to keep on giving extra auditory work to their school age child; the other describes work with teenagers who have had little auditory training before.

SEMPLE, Jean *Hearing Impaired Preschool Child*
Charles Thomas, 1970

Although not primarily an auditory approach, many of the suggestions and the advice are very useful to parents.

SHARP, Evelyn *Thinking is Child's Play*
Avon Paperbacks, 1969

Learning and teaching games for preschoolers, with an interesting introduction on the development of thinking in young children and how their ideas differ from our own.

STOTT, D.H. *The Parent as Teacher*
New Press, Toronto, 1972

This paperback is originally intended for parents of children with learning difficulties who want to help their children. It has helpful suggestions for dealing with some of the problems which arise when the parent has to take on the teacher role.

TAYLOR, Dorothy *Learning with Traditional Rhymes*
Ladybird Books, 1976

There are eight books in the series, graded from infants to school age children with actions to accompany each rhyme song. They are illustrated with photographs of childen playing the games as well as drawings to stimulate the imagination.

WHETNALL, Edith & Fry, D.B. *The Deaf Child*
Charles Thomas, 1972
Learning To Hear
Heinemann, 1970

Learning To Hear is an informational book about how hearing develops in both the deaf and the normal child and how deafness is determined and measured.
The Deaf Child reports on the auditory approach to training deaf children with other information relating to language development.

The HOME LIBRARY Books

These are regular children's books with simplified text, produced especially for children with language delay. A list of titles can be obtained from The Canadian Hearing Society, 60 Bedford Rd., Toronto, Canada, M5R 2K2.

VIDEOTAPES and CASSETTES

Learning to Listen in the Auditory Training Program at North York General Hospital with Warren Estabrooks and Pupils (1981) is a three-quarter-inch videotape showing auditory training with children from preschool age to early teens.

Conversations with Vanessa, John, Jonathan and Matthew is a cassette taped in June, 1980, of four of the *Learning to Listen* children in conversation with their parents.

Cassette tapes of VOICE programs with the following speakers: Helen Beebe, Marian Ernst, Leahea Grammatico, Doris Leckie, Daniel Ling, Ken Moses, Sister Nicholas, Winifred Northcott, Agnes Phillips (Ling), Doreen Pollack, and Father van Uden.

All the above are available through Voice for Hearing Impaired Children, P.O. Box 152, Station 'S', Toronto, Canada, M5M 4L7.

Glossary

AMPLIFICATION: Making sound louder especially by a hearing aid.

APHASIC: A condition where the child does not respond to sounds in speech, although testing as having normal hearing. A few aphasic children do respond to speech (can follow verbal instructions etc.) but are unable to make sensible sentences themselves.

APPROPRIATE USE OF LANGUAGE: Using words which relate to what is going on. Later, using the form of words expected in situations (e.g. "Shut-up" to other children but not to Grandma).

AUDIOGRAM: (See page 118, Part III). A chart for plotting the results of audiometric testing.

AUDIOMETRY (audiometric): The measuring of a person's response to sound in terms of pitch and loudness, compared with hearing response.

AUDIOLOGY (audiological): The science of testing to determine the amount and type of hearing loss; to make diagnosis on the degree of loss and to fit hearing aids.

AUDIOLOGIST: Describes a person trained to do this. A **qualified audiologist** is one whose qualifications are at university level. Many people do testing who are not so qualified—sometimes called audiological assistants, technicians, nurses, etc.

AUDITORY TRAINER: Any type of amplifier which is used to help develop the listening skills. It is generally used to describe a relatively small portable table instrument with headphones through which the pupil listens.

BABBLE: The sounds a young baby makes as vocal play, repeating one syllable over and over in different rhythms.

BINAURAL AIDS: Two separate aids or a special one-pack aid containing two sets of works. Each ear is stimulated. The rationale is that this almost duplicates the binaural effect of normal hearing.

BILATERAL DEAFNESS: This means that both ears are impaired. If only one ear is affected, the term **UNILATERAL DEAFNESS** is used.

BODY-TYPE AID: A hearing aid with a little box containing the microphone which is worn about chest level with a cord running to the receiver in the ear.

COMPREHENSION (speech or language): Understanding what is being said, even if all the words are not familiar.

COMPRESSION: A method of preventing excessively loud sounds from reaching the ear of a hearing aid user who requires a good deal of amplification in order to hear the quieter parts of speech. Methods of achieving this are **PEAK CLIPPING; AUTOMATIC VOLUME CONTROL (A.V.C.); LINEAR DYNAMIC RANGE COMPRESSION (D.R.C.).**

CONCEPT: The mental understanding of some relationships between objects and ideas in the child's world. Until the child has his concept e.g. "big" he will not be interested in the language needed to express it.

CONDUCTIVE LOSS: This is a hearing loss involving the middle ear. Any operations to date have been on people with this type of deafness. Children often have temporary conductive deafness after ear infections.

CONGENITAL DEAFNESS: The baby was born with a hearing loss. If he heard normally at birth and then lost hearing due to illness or some other cause, the term used is **ACQUIRED DEAFNESS.**

DISCRIMINATION: Being able to identify a sound or word as differing from another sound or word.

EAR LEVEL AIDS: Very small hearing aids which have the microphone included and are worn behind the ear. These are generally not so powerful as body-type, are more expensive and break more readily.

EARMOULD: The plastic insertion which fits on to the ear canal and to which the receiver is fastened (see diagram on page 126).

FEEDBACK: (1) The process of hearing one's own voice and using this to modify your own speech to match that of others.
(2) Auditory Feedback — The squeal produced when the microphone and receiver of a hearing aid are too close together. When an earmould does not fit properly allowing sound to escape this squeal will also occur.

HARD OF HEARING: Applied to a child, this means that the loss, although appreciable, is not so great that the child could not, unaided, develop some speech and language, although probably rather more slowly and inaccurately than normal. To an adult, in popular usage, it refers to anyone who has developed some hearing loss after having heard normally during the earlier years of life, no matter how great such a loss may be. In some areas the term used is **PARTIALLY DEAF.**

HEREDITARY DEAFNESS: Hearing impairment caused by a family trait carried down through the generations.

IMPRESSION (mould): The sound from the hearing aid receiver is carried into the ear by a plastic tube called the MOULD. This is made exactly to fit the ear. In order to achieve this, an impression of the ear canal is taken on a soft substance which later hardens. It is not easy to get a good impression from a child, but without one the hearing aid is inefficient so that the parents must be prepared to insist on proper fitting moulds. As the child grows, new moulds will have to be made.

JARGON: A stage of speech language development when the child "talks scribble". He makes what sounds like inflected sentences but they are verbal play and not intended to have meaning.

LANGUAGE: The way the child uses his vocabulary to express any situation. The grammatical organization of his speech. Language comprehension.

LIMITED HEARING: Hearing impairment.

LOCATING (localizing): The ability to identify the source of sound. This skill disappears with very slight hearing loss.

LOOP SYSTEM (inductive loop): A method of feeding a program from any electronic sound source, e.g. a television, into a hearing aid. The listener turns his aid to the "telephone" setting and can then receive the signal within the area of the loop which is a coil of wire connected to the sound source. A transformer is often needed to make the connection.

MASKING: If one ear is much better than the other, test sounds presented to the other ear might be heard by the good one and give a false result. A continuous sound is then applied to the better ear while the worse one is being tested. This allows the true threshold to be discovered.

MICROPHONE: The opening in a hearing aid through which the sound is admitted.

MONAURAL: A hearing aid which amplifies sound into one ear.

MULTIPLE HANDICAP: A child who has more than one abnormality, either physical, mental or a combination of both is said to be "multiply handicapped". For educational placement, a decision has to be made as to which is the major handicap and treatment is given for this, usually with some modification to accommodate the other handicap.

NERVE DEAFNESS: (Perceptive Deafness). Hearing impairment caused by some abnormality of the inner ear and/or the nerve connections to the brain. Sometimes called **SENSORY-NEURAL LOSS.**

ORAL/AURAL: An oral program for hearing impaired children with primary emphasis on auditory training rather than lipreading.

PROFOUNDLY DEAF: (See page 118, Part III). Deafness so great that a child could not be expected to learn to talk without help.

PROSTHETIC DEVICE: Anything worn to help overcome some bodily malfunction. With hearing impaired children, generally a hearing aid.

RECRUITMENT: A condition where the person with hearing impairment hears loud sounds almost as loudly as a normal person would, although quieter sounds are impaired. This, naturally, makes use of a hearing aid which amplifies all sounds extremely difficult.

RUBELLA DEAF: Hearing impairment caused by an attack of German measles during pregnancy. The virus can attack the unborn baby at the developmental stage or develop in the newly born after birth. A rubella deaf child is considered more likely to have multiple handicaps than are children whose deafness has other causes.

SENTENCE PATTERN: The long and short syllables plus the intonation and, usually, some of the vowel sounds in a sentence.

SEVERELY DEAF: (See page 118, Part III) A hearing loss which would make it very unlikely that a child could learn to speak without help. Any speech acquired without help would be very imperfect.

SPEECH: Actual sounds the child says. Speech may be said to be poor, although language is good—the child's pronunciation may be faulty but he is using his words in an appropriate manner.

SPONTANEOUS SPEECH: Speech which the child uses all by himself to comment on some situation; not merely repeating what his mother has just said.

STARTLE REFLEX: (Startle response) A very young baby will respond to a sudden loud noise by a convulsive jerk of the whole body. It is obviously not a very useful indication of hearing in the speech range.

TELEPHONE SWITCH: Some aids have a separate setting to be used with a telephone or a 'loop'. Sometimes other external speech (including his own feedback) is excluded by this; others have a mixed type switch bringing in both telephone and speech.

TONE SETTING: Most hearing aids can have their range altered slightly to bring in or cut out high frequency sounds.

VOCALIZE: The first speech sounds uttered by a baby. Often used to express any sound made by a child including babble, jargon and beginning speech.

VOLUME CONTROL: The mechanism in a hearing aid which makes the sound louder.

WHITE NOISE: A sound composed of all frequencies at the same volume. Often described as a "frying" sound. It is used in testing when masking and in some buildings to cover the general background noise.

Y - CORD: A monaural hearing aid with a cord split so receivers may be fitted into each ear. The sound received is considerably reduced by this technique and localization is not possible because each ear is getting sound from the same microphone.